YORK NOTES

General Editors: Professor A.N. Jeffares (*University of Stirling*) & Professor Suheil Bushrui (*American*

Geoffrey Chaucer

THE NUN'S PRIEST'S TALE

Notes by Anna Spackman

BA, MLITT (NEWCASTLE) DIPESL (LEEDS)

Tutorial Assistant, University of Dundee

LONGMAN
YORK PRESS

YORK PRESS
Immeuble Esseily, Place Riad Solh, Beirut

LONGMAN GROUP UK LIMITED
Longman House, Burnt Mill, Harlow,
Essex CM20 2JE, England
Associated companies, branches and representatives
throughout the world

First published 1980
Sixth impression 1993

ISBN 0-582-02290-8

Printed in Hong Kong
WC/04

Contents

Part 1

Introduction

Geoffrey Chaucer

The son of a wine merchant, Geoffrey Chaucer was born in London during the early 1340s, the exact year of his birth being unknown, and he died in London on 25 October 1400. During his life he served under three English kings and the comparative stability of his personal career must be seen against the continuation of the Hundred Years War between England and France, the terrible ravagings of the plague known as the Black Death and, in the latter part of his life, the civil upheavals of the reign of Richard II (1377–99), which ended in the King's deposition and murder by his cousin, Henry Bolingbroke, who subsequently became king.

Although many references to Chaucer and his family have been found in contemporary records, these are concerned mainly with business and legal transactions and with Chaucer's career as an administrative official of the Crown. Both Chaucer's father and grandfather had held appointments as collectors of custom dues on various goods and Chaucer's own career was to continue this pattern. The earliest known reference to Geoffrey Chaucer, in 1357, is in the household of the Countess of Ulster, wife of Lionel, third son of Edward III, where Chaucer probably served as a page. In this capacity he would have learnt correct social behaviour and good manners, as well as observing the administrative conduct of an aristocratic family. Also he would have been present at court functions and been acquainted with many important and influential people. In 1359 Chaucer was taken prisoner whilst serving on a military expedition in France and was released the following year, the King himself contributing money to the ransom. Later, in October 1360, Chaucer returned to France as a member of the Earl of Ulster's party at the peace negotiations between England and France, and he acted as a messenger carrying letters from Calais to England.

Whilst it is possible that Chaucer continued to be attached to the Ulster household during the early 1360s, there is no surviving information for this part of Chaucer's life. From 1366 material is available and there is much evidence both for Chaucer's journeys abroad, at times on diplomatic affairs, and for his administrative duties and services in London. From February to May 1366 Chaucer and three companions were granted a document of safe conduct by the King of Navarre to travel in Spain, possibly to join a military engagement. During the same year Chaucer appears to have married, as an annual grant for life of twelve marks was granted by Edward III to one Philippa Chaucer, a lady-in-waiting of the Queen in September 1366. By his marriage Chaucer ultimately became related to a powerful prince, John of Gaunt, whose third wife was Philippa's sister. Chaucer himself seems to have joined the royal household, as in June 1367 he received an annual grant of twenty marks for life, being described as a 'valettus' and 'esquire'. Throughout the following years there are frequent documentary references to the payments of these annuities and to gifts made to Chaucer and his wife as members of the royal household and the household of John of Gaunt.

In July 1368 Chaucer was granted a passport for foreign travel, but his destination is unknown. In the following year Chaucer may have been engaged on military service in France and in the summer of 1370 he was given letters of protection to travel abroad, but whether for military or diplomatic service is unclear. From December 1372 to May 1373 Chaucer travelled to Genoa as part of a mission to arrange an English port for Genoese ships, based upon peace and trade treaties confirmed between England and Genoa. Whilst in Italy Chaucer visited Florence and there is speculation as to whether he may have met the famous Italian poets, Petrarch and Boccaccio. It does seem probable that Chaucer knew Italian and this may explain why he was chosen to investigate a Genoese ship held near London in 1373. During the next fourteen years Chaucer was sent on frequent foreign diplomatic missions: in 1376 he accompanied Sir John de Burley, probably overseas; between February 1377 and March 1381 he travelled in connection with peace negotiations between France and England and a marriage negotiation of Richard II to a French princess; from May to September 1378 he visited Lombardy and in 1387 he made a trip to Calais.

Although Chaucer was employed frequently as a diplomat, his main administrative post, which he acquired in June 1374, was as a Controller of the Wool Custom and Subsidy in the Port of London. This office was confirmed by Richard II on his accession to the throne in 1377. Probably in 1382 Chaucer also became Controller of the Petty Custom. In 1377, 1378, 1383 and 1384 Chaucer requested the appointment of a deputy whilst he was abroad and to help with extra work, and in 1385 he requested and was allowed a permanent deputy. Throughout his service as a customs official from 1374–86, Chaucer leased a dwelling above one of London's gates at Aldgate, a noisy and possibly dangerous place to live. Also during this time there is evidence of his acting in legal positions as a surety and a guardian.

From 1385–9 Chaucer served as a Justice of the Peace for the county of Kent and in 1386 he was elected as a Member of Parliament for Kent. In the same year he was replaced as Controller of Customs and it is probable that Philippa died in the following year, as there are no further payments made to her after June 1387. With the failure of the Court party to remain influential, Chaucer suffered a period of neglect but in 1389, on the regaining of control by the King, he was appointed to the post of Clerk of the Works, which he held until 1391. In this administrative post he was responsible for the maintenance of certain royal properties and accounting duties. In June 1391 he was made a sub-forester of the King's park at North Petherton. In February 1384 Chaucer was granted a life annuity of twenty pounds by Richard II in recognition of his good services and, in December 1397, a yearly tun of wine. After his accession in 1399, Henry IV confirmed the grants with the addition of forty marks. In December of the same year Chaucer leased a tenement at Westminster Abbey for fifty-three years but he died in the following autumn, traditionally on 25 October 1400. He was buried in the Abbey, a church more normally used for royal burials.

From these selective biographical details it can be seen that references to Chaucer reveal only his administrative and economic affairs with few glimpses of his personal life and none at all of his creative life.

Literary background

In the late fourteenth century Chaucer wrote sophisticated poetry in English for a courtly audience, yet this development was one of comparatively recent origin. In 1066 England was invaded and conquered by William, the Duke of Normandy in northern France, and thus became a country ruled by a French-speaking aristocracy. For the next two hundred years French was the dominant language, the language of government, culture and polite usage. Latin was the language of the Church, used for all its functions and for scholarly works, and the language of higher government. English became dissociated with any general cultural expression. It seems probable that a knowledge of French and English was a social distinction, French being spoken by those of the aristocracy and those with social aspirations, whilst English, although the language of the majority, was the language of the socially inferior.

During this time a considerable amount of French literature was produced in England for the entertainment of the English court and aristocracy. This introduced into England many new forms of poetry with new ideas and subjects very different from the epic and Christian concerns of Old English poetry. French culture was influential throughout Europe and the Anglo-Norman literature of England demonstrates the new forms, such as romance, and the new subjects, such as the values of knighthood and the conduct of love. Simultaneously, the intellectual vigour of the country is reflected in the number of Latin writers of the twelfth and thirteenth centuries, many of whom studied on the Continent. Such English writings as do survive are mainly religious or instructional, although some evidence suggests the limited continuation of the older verse forms. It is also obvious that much popular entertainment in verse and song was conveyed in English, but such oral forms have left little trace.

During the thirteenth century, partly because of the severing of the close relationship between England and France, the situation began to alter and English became eventually the common language, greatly enriched by the addition of many French words. For some considerable time French maintained its control as an administrative and cultural language, but in polite circles French became increasingly a cultivated language, not an inherited one. The wider use of English is shown by the number of romances being adapted to or written in English, and official use of French reveals at times an imperfect knowledge of the language. Despite efforts to halt the decline of French, the use of English increased and the Hundred Years War between England and France, the emergence of a middle class and the betterment of many English speakers helped in the adoption of English generally in the fourteenth century.

A knowledge of French continued amongst the educated and cultured and Chaucer himself is an indication of this. Richard II owned French books and Chaucer's friend, John Gower (c. 1330–1408), wrote a lengthy French poem. French culture still continued to be an influential factor in the literature produced in England, especially by Chaucer, yet the literary climate had altered and during the late fourteenth century English literature flourished. The re-emergence of English as a literary language reflects its disuse as such. There was then no standard language, in contrast to both the end of the Old English period and the present day. Authors wrote in their own dialects, which reflected their different pronunciations and vocabularies. Chaucer's own dialect was a major ancestor of Modern English and is more accessible to us than those of many other extant medieval texts. Such poems as *Sir Gawain and the Green Knight* and *Piers Plowman* are as different from each other as they are from Chaucer's works. English verse reflected the influence of France in form and vocabulary and displayed the re-emergence of the old alliterative metre, which owed nothing to France.

Other historical factors influenced English poetry at this time. The presentation of poetry seems to have been mainly by oral delivery, partly because poetry was a form of public entertainment, partly because most people were illiterate, but also because of the difficulty of dissemination. Before the introduction of printing, book production was in manuscript form, copied by scribes, which made the process lengthy and costly. Oral presentation was a speedier way to reach a wider audience, whose ability to listen and comprehend was more developed than a contemporary literate audience. Most probably Chaucer read his poems to a court audience or to a group of friends, although it is possible that he circulated his writings in manuscript for private reading. This public presentation has been judged by some critics to account for some of the sophistication and charm of Chaucer's poetry. He can address his audience directly, involve them in his poem and play games with them in the form of an assumed character.

Chaucer and his friends were examples of a new type of author, already in evidence on the Continent, the literate layman. For a long time literacy had been the prerogative of the clergy and a few of the laity, but the development of an administration not dominated by clerics and the increasing education of the bourgeoisie produced men like Chaucer—educated, learned, and lay. It is significant that we know Chaucer by name and can identify a body of literature with him, for the bulk of medieval literature is anonymous. Chaucer was recognised by his contemporaries as a poet as three compliments and various imitations during his lifetime suggest. The fourteenth century saw the development of the awareness of poets of their individuality as authors, not merely as entertainers, and Chaucer's poetry fully reflects this awareness.

Chaucer's writings

Whether or not Chaucer had any formal education, his love of reading and acquiring information is evident throughout his work. His wide knowledge of the classics and learned works such as Boethius's *Consolation of Philosophy* (see p.10), of French and Italian poetry is demonstrated by Chaucer's use of them in his own works. In his method of adapting and using the material of other writers, Chaucer displays the medieval attitude towards authorship. Originality of subject matter was not considered necessary, as it is today, and authors used and reworked material from all available sources. To claim such sources gave the new work an added prestige and it seems that, at times, sources were invented for this purpose. Throughout his work Chaucer used and acknowledged his sources, but this traditional acknowledgement gave him the opportunity for mischievous manipulation. At times he denies authorial responsibility for his characters' actions and words by claiming he must follow his source, and, when claiming to follow his source most closely, he invents new material. So Chaucer used existing stories and forms to create new works with subtle differences and interpretations. Whether Chaucer's audience knew his sources and could recognise the alterations is hard to decide, but such comparisons make a fascinating study for modern scholars.

The definite chronology of Chaucer's works is not known, but it seems probable that those poems which show most clearly the influence of French poetry are the earliest. Given the current cultural conditions, Chaucer must have become acquainted with the poetry of the famous French poets, Machaut, Froissart and Deschamps. Their influence is shown not only by echoes of their poems, but in Chaucer's choice of the dream-vision form and the subject of love. A translation of a French poem, *An ABC*, appears to be an early work and it is possible that Chaucer may have translated part of *Le Roman de la Rose*, a twelfth-century French poem of great influence. This dream-vision poem is an account of falling in love, told through the medium of allegory and portraying the exquisite emotions of love. Even if the Middle English translation is not Chaucer's, he knew the poem, and this and other French poetry clearly influenced him. His earliest major poem is probably *The Book of the Duchess*, written on the death of Blanche, the first wife of John of Gaunt. Blanche died in 1369, so Chaucer's first poetic attempts can be dated to the late 1360s or early 1370s. Chaucer was never wholly uninfluenced by love of French poetry and the use of its forms and subjects, but his capabilities were developed by his acquaintance with the Italian and Latin works of Dante (1265–1321), Petrarch (1304–74) and Boccaccio (1313–75). From the early 1370s to the mid-1380s Chaucer wrote a substantial number of works which reflect this Italian interest and show his developing maturity. Both *The House of Fame* and *The Parliament of Fowls*, although dream-visions, show Italian influence and both *Troilus and Criseyde* and *Palamon and Arcite*, later to become *The Knight's Tale*, are modelled on poems by Boccaccio. During this time he also translated Boethius's *Consolation of Philosophy* from Latin into the English *Boece*, and probably wrote other peoms based on Italian and Latin models which were included later in *The Canterbury Tales*.

The dream-visions, in which the narrator himself is an actor, the great romances, and the translations, all reflect Chaucer's wide variety of interests and concerns. In his later years he worked on two structurally similar poems, *The Legend of Good Women* and *The Canterbury Tales*. *The Legend* has a prologue in the form of a dream-vision, in which the narrator is given a penance by the god of love as a punishment for his defamation of women in *Troilus and Criseyde*. He is to write stories of women who have been constant in love. The poem remains unfinished, breaking off after the tenth tale of a good woman. The poem is of interest, partly because there are two versions of the prologue and partly because it shows the earlier use of the structure of a prologue and a series of tales. Although the prologues are lively and of great charm, the stories, all demonstrating the same quality, do not interest. Possibly Chaucer realised from this that variety of tales and tellers was necessary to sustain such a structure. Certainly *The Canterbury Tales* avoids the monotony of the earlier poem.

The Canterbury Tales, Chaucer's most popular work, remains incomplete and unrevised. The scale of the work, if we accept the Host's words, is monumental—two tales by each pilgrim on the outward and return journey. Even in its existing form it is clear that this pattern is not maintained. Such a pilgrim as the Nun's Priest, whom we know little of from *The General Prologue*, tells a tale, and a traveller who joins the pilgrims later, the Canon's Yeoman, also contributes. There are unfinished tales, interrupted tales and the only character to tell even two tales is Chaucer the pilgrim. The order of the tales is not clearly established, for they have survived as a series of unrelated fragments, the most favoured manuscript order not suiting the topographical references. Yet *The Canterbury Tales* is a rewarding work, because fundamentally none of these difficulties affects a consideration of the tales themselves.

The device of the framed collection of stories is widespread and of ancient origin, but the choice of a pilgrimage as a framework provided Chaucer with a most flexible form. It allowed him to present a wide variety of people of differing characters and backgrounds, united by a common motivation. The variety of people would ensure a variety of tales and *The Canterbury Tales* displays many of the most popular medieval literary genres: romances, fabliaux, saints' lives, didactic tales, devotional writings and so on. In *The Monk's Tale* there is even an example of a collection of stories on the theme of tragedy. Also the framework allowed internal dramatic development. Certain rivalries and animosities develop amongst the pilgrims and tales are told to score off other tellers. Yet, however realistic the reactions in the links, however realistic the illusion the pilgrimage gives, *The Canterbury Tales* is a fiction, not an account of an actual pilgrimage. The tales are of major importance and the relationship between the tales, how they illumine and define each other, is the chief concern.

The Nun's Priest's Tale is the last tale in Fragment VII, following *The Monk's Tale*, which is preceded by the tales of the Shipman, the Prioress and the two tales told by Chaucer the pilgrim. In essence these six tales show the variety and contrast employed throughout *The Canterbury Tales*. First, the Shipman tells a racy fabliau, a bawdy, domestic tale of a merchant, his wife and a monk which is contrasted with the Prioress's pious tale of the boy martyr. Then, Chaucer the pilgrim offers a jolly popular romance, (probably a literary parody), which is halted by the Host because it is so bad. Instead, he tells the lengthy didactic prose tale of Melibee. The Monk follows this instructional work with a series of tales exemplifying the concept of tragedy. He, too, is interrupted and his dreary catalogue is followed by the merry, 'almost' tragedy of Chauntecleer. Contrast is evident in the different characters of the tellers and their occupations. Two, the Shipman and Chaucer, are laymen and three, the Prioress, the Monk, and the Nun's Priest, are clerics. The subject matter of their tales reflects these differences. The Shipman's fabliau is concerned with the comfortable middle-class world, the Prioress's story reflects the idealised conditions of a martyrdom, Chaucer's romance of Sir Thopas portrays an equally idealised, though fairy, world and his story of Melibee is a didactic allegory. The variety of great figures mentioned by the Monk includes real people, and the concluding tale is of birds and animals. This subject contrast is reflected in the different styles. *The Shipman's Tale* and *The Nun's Priest's Tale* are written in rhyming couplets, *The Prioress's Tale* and *The Monk's Tale* are written in seven and eight line stanzas respectively, *The Tale of Sir Thopas* is presented in a burlesque of the metrical romance stanza, and *The Tale of Melibee* is in prose. Three of the tales are told for our enjoyment, whilst the remaining three, those of the Monk and the Prioress and the *Melibee*, are told for our edification. Three of the tales show the relationship of marriage: the Shipman deals with trickery and deceit, the *Melibee* is a Christian allegory, and Chauntecleer and Pertelote demonstrate domestic tension and happiness.

By contrast and comparison our enjoyment is increased, but the majority of the tales can be appreciated individually. The charm and gaiety of *The Nun's Priest's Tale* is enhanced by following the tedious tale of the Monk, and the gentle mocking of the tragic theme in the tale of the cock and the fox increases our human awareness. So the greatness of *The Canterbury Tales* can be seen both in its overall design and in its individual components, the tales. Familiarity can only breed greater wonder and pleasure.

A note on the text

Although no manuscripts of Chaucer's poetry exist from his own lifetime, many fifteenth-century manuscripts do survive. The first printing of *The Canterbury Tales*, including *The Nun's Priest's Tale*, was carried out by William Caxton in 1478 and again in 1484. He and subsequent printers also printed separate editions of other works, and it was not until 1532 that an attempt to print a complete edition of Chaucer's works was made by William Thynne.

All references are to the edition of *The Nun's Priest's Tale* in *The Complete Works of Geoffrey Chaucer*, edited by F.N. Robinson, second edition, Oxford University Press, London, 1957. The glossary and notes are greatly indebted to two excellent single editions: *The Nun's Priest's Tale*, edited by Kenneth Sisam, Oxford University Press, Oxford, 1927, and *The Nun's Priest's Tale*, edited by Nevill Coghill and Christopher Tolkien, Harrap, London, 1959.

In the glossary all words not having their modern form or meaning are glossed on their first appearance. The exception are those words in which the substitution of 'i' for 'y' will produce the modern form.

Part 2

Summaries
of THE NUN'S PRIEST'S TALE

A general summary

The Nun's Priest's Tale follows the account of a number of tragic stories told by the Monk as his contribution to the pilgrims' entertainment. The Monk is one of two contributors who are interrupted in their story-telling and prevented from finishing their tales. For the Knight, who is described in *The General Prologue* as

> nevere yet no vileynye ne sayde
> In al his lyf unto no maner wight.   (70-1)

breaks in upon the Monk's rendering

> good sire, namoore of this!
> That ye han seyd is right ynough, ywis,
> And muchel moore; for litel hevynesse
> Is right ynough to muche folk, I gesse.   (2767–70)

The Host also expresses his dislike of the tragic mode and the impracticability of lamenting over past pain. Instead the Host, who claims that he has been prevented from falling asleep only by the noise of the bridle bells decorating the Monk's horse, invites 'daun Piers' to 'sey somwhat of huntyng'. The Monk is offended by this trivial request and refuses to entertain his fellow pilgrims with a light-hearted tale.

The Host turns to the Nun's Priest and instructs him to 'telle us swich thyng as may oure hertes glade'. For, despite the poor appearance of his horse, so long as the animal is serviceable the Priest should be happy and contented. Good-humouredly the Nun's Priest agrees to the request and 'this sweete preest, this goodly man sir John' embarks upon his tale of the cock, Chauntecleer and the hen, Pertelote.

The tale, which is the familiar one of the cock who is tricked by the fox who himself is tricked subsequently by the cock, is retold by Chaucer in an expanded form which reflects Chaucer's own literary and intellectual interests. For, whilst the traditional plot remains, it is elaborated by discussions on many topics which Chaucer weaves into his tale to develop the characters and to enrich the moral implications of his story. Whilst retaining the figures of the birds, Chauntecleer and Pertelote,

Chaucer also gives them the easily recognisable personalities of a man and a woman, combining the romantic attachment of a lover and his lady with the more prosaic and practical relationship between a husband and a wife.

In brief, the tale is concerned with the adventures of Chauntecleer and Pertelote, who belong to a poor widow whose live-stock consists of three sows, three cows and a sheep in addition to the poultry in the yard. Life for the birds is comfortable until one morning Chauntecleer groaning in his sleep alarms his favourite wife, Pertelote, who inquires what it is that distresses her husband. In answer Chauntecleer recounts his dream in which a dog-like creature of a yellowish-red colour appearing in the yard wished to kill him and whose bright eyes alarmed the cock and caused him to groan. Pertelote is aghast to discover that her husband is a coward so easily frightened by a mere dream. Dreams, in her explanation, are caused by bodily disorders and she counsels her husband to take a laxative which will purge him physically and thus relieve the conditions which produce frightening dreams.

Chauntecleer, whilst grateful for her concern, is somewhat contemptuous of her ignorance as he believes that dreams do have a greater significance and are not simply the result of a physical upset. Dreams, if properly understood, can be indicative of future happiness or distress and the cock quotes at length two stories which illustrate the tragic results of ignoring dreams. He supports his belief with a further example drawn from the legend of an English saint and numerous biblical and classical references. Having displayed his intellectual superiority Chauntecleer comforts himself with the excellence of his wife and their life of happiness together, and, fortified by his refusal to take a laxative, he resumes his normal farmyard duties.

Later in the day, 3 May, Chauntecleer is enjoying the spring and all its attendant associations of love and joy, when his good fortune is disturbed. A fox, living close by for three years, has broken into the yard and is hidden in a bed of plants watching the farmyard activities and waiting to seize the cock. The mild spring weather and a feeling of well-being encourage the birds to enjoy themselves but suddenly Chauntecleer sees the fox and instinctively gives a warning cry. Preparing to run away, Chauntecleer is prevented by the courteous words of the fox who declares his friendship for the cock. He says that he intends the bird no harm for he has been attracted to the yard to hear Chauntecleer's singing. Claiming acquaintance with Chauntecleer's parents the fox praises both Chauntecleer's own and his father's singing. He explains to Chauntecleer that his father, to improve his voice, would close his eyes, stand on tip-toe and stretch out his neck. In both wisdom and musical ability there was nobody in the area to surpass him. The fox requests Chauntecleer to sing so that he can judge whether he is as good as his father.

Chauntecleer, completely deceived by the fox's kind words and flattery, does as his father did and crows with his eyes tightly closed. Immediately the fox, Russell, seizes the bird and carries him off to the wood and safety. However the alarm is raised by the frightened hens and Pertelote in particular screams so loudly that the widow and her daughters come out into the yard and see the fox with his burden. The hue and cry goes up and all the available people and dogs pursue the wicked fox. Alarmed by the barking dogs and shouting people, the cows and pigs join the chase. Even the ducks and geese are frightened by the noise and add to the confusion as do a swarm of bees equally disturbed by the outcry. To increase the noise musical instruments are fetched and the 'poops' and 'toots' complete the range of human, animal and bird cries.

Meanwhile Chauntecleer suggests fearfully to the fox that he should turn to the following crowd and tell them to go home as now that the fox has reached the wood the cock is beyond saving. Proud of his success the fox agrees to do so. Immediately he opens his mouth Chauntecleer escapes from him and flies up into a tree. Realising his mistake the fox tries to persuade the cock to come down, explaining that Chauntecleer has misunderstood his intentions. Chauntecleer, assessing only too accurately Russell's murderous desires, refuses to be tricked again and blames himself for lack of foresight. Similarly, having been thwarted in his attempt, the fox reproves himself for not having kept his mouth closed.

The two main characters having drawn their conclusions and morals on their own conduct, the narrator suggests that the pilgrims should consider the deeper moral significance of the tale of the fox and the cock and of the cock and the hen.

In an epilogue to the tale the Host expresses his approval both of the 'mery tale' and of the teller. He awards the Nun's Priest his highest compliment by suggesting that if he were not a priest and thus celibate he would be a lusty and demanding lover as evidenced by his physical appearance in addition to his tale.

Detailed summaries

Lines 2767-820

Throughout *The Canterbury Tales* the individual stories are linked by passages which serve as prologues and epilogues to the tales. These links can take the form of a conversation between the pilgrims, the Host as master of ceremonies being a prominent participant. In this prologue the Knight, growing weary of the unhappy and tedious recital of tragic stories, requests the Monk not to continue and expresses his preference for tales of prosperity. The Host is in agreement, although his bluntly expressed view of the tragedies is in contrast with the Knight's more general reservation. The Host, in his vigorous and colloquial speech, demands a livelier tale but he has offended the Monk by his criticisms and the Monk declines to tell another tale.

In no way abashed the Host turns to another cleric, the Nun's Priest. Apart from a brief reference to 'preestes thre' in the description of the Prioress in *The General Prologue* this is the first awareness we have of this pilgrim. From the remarks of the Host we learn that the priest rides a worn-out horse but despite this discomfort the Host encourages the priest to be cheerful. Agreeing that unless he is cheerful he will be disapproved of, the Nun's Priest starts his story.

NOTES AND GLOSSARY

quod:	said
sire:	sir
namoore:	no more
that:	what
ye:	you (plural subject form used in formal speech or by an inferior to a superior)
han:	have
seyd:	said
right:	quite
ynough:	enough
ywis:	indeed
muchel:	much
moore:	more
litel:	little
hevynesse:	sadness
muche:	many
gesse:	think
seye:	say

greet:	great
disese:	distress
welthe:	wealth
ese:	comfort
heere(n):	to hear
hire:	their (plural possessive pronoun)
sodeyn:	sudden
fal:	fall
allas:	alas
contrarie:	opposite
joye:	joy
solas:	consolation
whan:	when
hath:	has
povre:	poor
estaat:	rank
wexeth:	grows
fortunat:	successful
prosperitee:	prosperity
swich:	such (a)
gladsom:	pleasant
it thynketh me:	it seems to me
were:	would be
goodly:	proper
for to telle:	to tell
ye:	yes
oure:	our
Hooste:	host, the landlord of the Tabard Inn, Southwark, where the pilgrims met to start their journey. He accompanies them and it is his suggestion that the pilgrims should tell tales to pass the journey
seint Poules:	Saint Paul's Cathedral, the largest London church
belle:	bell
sooth:	truth
clappeth:	talks (the hammer in a bell is a clapper)
lowde:	loudly
spak:	spoke
clowde:	cloud
noot:	do not know (ne woot)
nevere:	not at all
als:	also
tragedie:	tragedy

right:	just
herde:	heard
pardee:	by God, assuredly
remedie:	remedy
biwaille:	to bewail
ne:	nor
compleyne:	to lament
doon:	done
peyne:	distress
yow:	you (non-subject form)
blesse:	bless
youre:	your
anoyeth:	annoys
al:	all
compaignye:	company
nat:	not
boterflye:	butterfly
therinne:	in that
ther:	there
desport:	amusement
wherfore:	and so
daun:	master (title of respect)
hertely:	with all my heart
somwhat:	something
elles:	else
sikerly:	certainly
nere:	were it not (for) (ne were)
that:	which
bridel:	bridle
hange:	hang
hevene kyng:	the King of heaven, Christ
alle:	all
dyde:	died
sholde:	should
er:	before
doun:	down
for:	on account of
slough:	muddy hole
thanne:	then
hadde:	had
toold:	told
in veyn:	pointlessly

certeinly:	certainly
as that:	as
thise:	these
clerkes:	scholars
seyn:	say
whereas:	where
noon:	no
noght:	not
sentence:	opinion
wel:	well
woot:	know
substance:	the innate power
shal:	shall
sey:	tell (imperative)
preye:	beg
nay:	no
lust:	desire
pleye:	to amuse
lat:	let (imperative)
speche:	words
boold:	bold
Nonnes:	nun's
Preest:	priest
anon:	immediately
com:	come (imperative)
neer:	near
thou:	you (singular subject form used in familiar relationships and in speaking to inferiors)
hyder:	here
hertes:	hearts
glade:	gladden
blithe:	gay
jade:	worn-out horse
thogh:	though
thyn:	your
hors:	horse
bothe:	both
foul:	dirty
lene:	thin
wol:	will
thee:	you (singular non-subject form)
rekke nat a bene:	do not care a bean: do not worry

looke:	see (imperative)
murie:	cheerful
everemo:	always
yis:	yes
moot:	may
go:	walk
but:	unless
attamed:	begun on
everichon:	every one
sweete:	amiable
goodly:	worthy

Lines 2821–46

The tale opens with a description of the living conditions of the 'povre wydwe', the owner of the cock, Chauntecleer and the hen, Pertelote. The elderly woman lives in a small cottage beside a grove of trees in a valley. Her circumstances are reflected in her scanty possessions and the conditions in which she lives. She supports herself and her two daughters by careful economy and she owns three sows, three cows and a sheep called Malle. Her house is sooty as a result of an open fire and her diet is not one of delicate food flavoured with tasty sauces for she can only afford milk and brown bread with an occasional egg or piece of bacon which she has produced herself.

In this opening paragraph the narrator stresses the simplicity of the widow's way of life through contrast with the diet and manners of more wealthy and noble people. This is expressed through the vocabulary which is more normally applied to other social classes. A 'bour' and 'halle' are parts of a castle, applicable to the description of a noble lady but not of a poor widow. 'Poynaunt sauce' and 'deyntee morsel' are parts of a noble, not a poor, meal. Over-eating does not make the widow ill for she eats sparingly because of her poverty and this and exercise result in her peace of mind. She does not suffer from the gout or apoplexy, two diseases caused by excessive drinking of wine. In fact, she drinks no wine at all but eats and drinks according to her means and what her skill as a dairy woman produces.

The narrator, whilst describing the restricted means of the widow, alludes to a different way of life through his examples. Thus the effect is not one of harshness and ugliness but rather a want of graciousness and beauty. The widow lives a dignified and hard-working life which results in a means of livelihood but which cannot provide excesses of wealth. By his use of words more frequently used in tales of noble life, the narrator prepares the reader for their use in the descriptions of Chauntecleer and Pertelote. Similarly the discussion of the poor widow's diet will be reflected in the discussion of the birds' diet.

NOTES AND GLOSSARY

wydwe:	widow
somdeel:	somewhat
stape:	advanced
whilom:	formerly
narwe:	confined, small
cotage:	cottage, small house of a peasant
biside:	beside
grove:	group of trees
stondynge:	standing
dale:	valley
syn:	since
thilke:	the same (the ilke)
wyf:	wife (since the day her husband died)
pacience:	patience
ladde:	led
ful:	very
lyf:	life
hir:	her (possessive feminine pronoun)
catel:	property
rente:	income
housbondrie:	economical use, thrift
hire:	her (object pronoun)
sente:	sent
foond:	provided for
hirself:	herself
doghtren:	daughters
thre:	three
sowes:	sows
keen:	cows
highte:	named
Malle:	diminutive form of female name, Mary
bour:	small private room in a large house or castle
halle:	large common living-room in a castle or house (the poultry live here in this tale—cf. 2884). The narrator uses such words as 'catel' and 'rente' and 'bour' and 'halle' in his description of the widow's property in a humorously exaggerated fashion
eet:	ate

sklendre:	frugal
meel:	meal
poynaunt:	sharp-flavoured
hir neded never:	she had no need
a deel:	a bit (she had no need of a sharp-flavoured sauce)
deyntee:	delicate
thurgh:	through
throte:	throat
diete:	food, diet
accordant:	in keeping with
cote:	cottage
repleccioun:	over-eating
ne:	not
nevere:	never
sik:	ill
attempree:	moderate
phisik:	medicine (a moderate diet was her only treatment)
hertes suffisaunce:	contentment of heart
goute:	gout; an inflammation of the toe joints, associated with over-drinking
lette:	prevented . . . from
nothyng:	not at all
daunce:	dance
n'apoplexie:	apoplexy; an arrest of motion and intellect caused by a rush of blood to the head (ne apoplexie)
shente:	injured
heed:	head
wyn:	wine
whit:	white
reed:	red
bord:	table
moost:	mostly
blak:	black
broun breed:	brown bread, rye bread
lak:	shortage
seynd:	grilled
bacoun:	bacon
somtyme:	sometimes
ey:	egg
tweye:	two
maner:	kind of
deye:	dairy woman

Lines 2847–81

In the following passage the widow's prize possession and the hero of the story, Chauntecleer the cock, is introduced. The narrator describes him with all the attributes of a bird, with his crowing, his comb, his bill, his legs, toes and claws. Likewise in his behaviour he is a bird, being the only cock amongst seven hens. However, as with the description of the widow, the vocabulary which is used in the depiction both of the appearance and conduct of the cock and of Pertelote suggests a world far removed from the farmyard. Such words as 'gentil', 'governaunce', 'plesaunce', 'paramours' and the description of Pertelote are appropriate to a romance description of aristocratic lords and ladies. Chauntecleer and Pertelote behave as noble lovers, whose formality of address and behaviour towards each other demonstrates the nobility of their love. However, the narrator does not let the reader forget that his characters are birds and the humour arises from the application of an elevated style of description to the appearance and behaviour of poultry. The device of talking birds and animals is a familiar one in such fables but in *The Nun's Priest's Tale* the power of human speech seems to arise naturally from the details of the descriptions.

The other main aspects of this passage are firstly, the contrast which is presented between the colourful and gracious portraits of the named Chauntecleer and Pertelote and that of the anonymous 'povre wydwe': secondly, the emphasis which the narrator places upon Chauntecleer's great ability to crow, a feature which plays a significant part in the later action of the story.

NOTES AND GLOSSARY

yeerd:	yard, enclosure
aboute:	round
stikkes:	stakes
drye:	dry
dych:	ditch
withoute:	on the outside
cok:	cock
Chauntecleer:	'the clear singer'; the cock's name demonstrates his most notable quality
nas:	was not (ne was)
peer:	equal
voys:	voice
murier:	more delightful
orgon:	organ, a keyboard instrument used in churches

messe-dayes:	mass days, festivals of the Church year on which Christians must go to a church service, the mass
gon:	plays
wel:	much
sikerer:	more trustworthy
logge:	dwelling
clokke:	clock
orlogge:	clock
nature:	instinct
ech:	each
ascencioun:	a rising over the horizon
equynoxial:	celestial equator; any point on the equator was supposed to make a circuit of 360° in 24 hours
toun:	town
degrees:	degrees
fiftene:	fifteen; a point on the celestial equator appeared to move 15° each hour. Chauntecleer, by instinct, knew the movement of the 'equynoxial' and crew every hour when a further 15° appeared over the horizon
weren:	were
ascended:	risen over the horizon
myghte:	could
amended:	improved
coomb:	comb
the fyn:	the finest
batailled:	crenellated
castel:	castle
wal:	wall
byle:	bill
jeet:	jet
shoon:	shone
lyk:	like
asure:	azure, bright blue
legges:	legs
toon:	toes
nayles:	claws
whitter:	more white
lylye flour:	lily flower
burned:	burnished
gentil:	well-bred, noble
governaunce:	control

sevene:	seven
hennes:	hens
doon:	to do
plesaunce:	pleasure
sustres:	sisters
paramours:	mistresses
wonder:	wondrously
faireste:	most beautifully
hewed:	coloured
cleped:	called
faire:	beautiful
damoysele:	mistress (form of address)
curteys:	courteous, having the manners of the court
discreet:	circumspect
debonaire:	gentle
compaignable:	friendly
bar:	bore
faire:	well
oold:	old
trewely:	truly
in hoold:	in keeping
loken:	secured
lith:	limb
wel:	happiness
hym:	to him
therwith:	through it
hem:	them
synge:	sing
brighte:	bright
sonne:	sun
gan (for) to:	began to
sprynge:	to rise
sweete:	sweet
accord:	harmony

'My lief is faren in londe': 'My love has gone away', possibly a line from a popular song

tyme:	time
understonde:	understood
beestes:	animals
briddes:	birds
koude:	could
speke:	speak

Lines 2882–907

One morning Chauntecleer wakes disturbed by a dream and, on a concerned enquiry from Pertelote, he tells her of what has made him groan. He has dreamt that a russet-coloured animal with black-tipped ears and tail and with glowing eyes wanted to kill him in the farmyard.

The birds address each other with great courtesy and are made to sound like human lovers speaking in a romance.

NOTES AND GLOSSARY

so bifel:	it so happened
in a dawenynge:	one day at dawn
wyves:	wives
perche:	perch
gan gronen:	groaned
dreem:	dream
drecched:	troubled
soore:	sorely
roore:	cry out
agast:	frightened
deere:	dear
eyleth:	troubles
manere:	way
been:	are
verray:	fine
sleper:	sleeper
answerde:	answered
Madame:	Madame (form of address)
agrief:	amiss
me mette:	it came to me in a dream, I dreamt
meschief:	trouble
yet:	still
myn:	my
afright:	afraid
swevene:	dream
recche:	interpret
aright:	favourably
kepe:	keep
prisoun:	prison
romed:	walked
doun:	down
withinne:	in
wheer as:	where

saugh:	saw
wolde:	would
maad:	made
areest:	seizure
deed:	dead
bitwixe:	between
yelow:	yellow
eeris:	ears
unlyk:	unlike
remenant:	rest
heeris:	hairs, pelt
snowte:	snout
smal:	thin
glowynge:	glowing
eyen:	eyes
feere:	fear
almoost:	almost
deye:	die
gronyng:	groaning
doutelees:	assuredly

Lines 2908–69

On hearing Chauntecleer's dream Pertelote is astonished at her husband's lack of courage and is ashamed that she has loved such a coward. Only brave, wise, generous and discreet men can expect to be loved by women, who value these qualities and not those of a coward and a boaster. Pertelote tells Chauntecleer that he should not have been so un-loverlike as to tell his beloved of his fears and, although 'he may appear brave, he has no manly heart as he is afraid of dreams.

Having upbraided Chauntecleer for his lack of manly and courteous behaviour, Pertelote goes on to explain to Chauntecleer that his dream has no meaning to be afraid of but is simply the result of physical disorders. An excess of bile 'rede colera' is causing Chauntecleer to dream about red objects just as an excess of melancholy will cause the sufferer to dream of black objects. She concludes her informed medical discussion by quoting from the moral sayings ascribed to the author, Cato, to take no heed of dreams. Instead Pertelote recommends that Chauntecleer should purge his body by taking a laxative to help his bowel movements. As there is no doctor Pertelote herself will instruct Chauntecleer what to do and what he should eat. She is convinced that he can be restored to health easily and quickly and that he need fear no more dreams. Pertelote has reduced Chauntecleer's terror to nothing more than the need for a laxative.

NOTES AND GLOSSARY

avoy!:	shame!
hertelees:	faint heart
kan:	can
feith:	faith
certes:	indeed
what so:	whatever
womman:	woman
seith:	says
desiren:	desire
myghte:	may
bee:	be
housbondes:	husbands
hardy:	bold
free:	generous
secree:	discreet
nygard:	niggard
agast:	terrified
tool:	weapon
avauntour:	braggart
dorste:	dared
myghte:	could
aferd:	afraid
mannes:	of a man
berd:	beard
konne:	can
woot:	knows
vanitee:	illusion
sweven:	dreaming
engendren:	spring (from)
replecciouns:	excess of humours. From 2923 onwards Pertelote gives her reason as to the cause of Chauntecleer's dream. She believes that the balance of the body's humours or fluids has been upset. An individual's temperament or 'compleccioun' results from the mixture of the four humours, blood, phlegm, melancholy or black bile and choler or red bile. Chauntecleer has dreamt of a red and black object, therefore, according to the hen's diagnosis, he is suffering from a surfeit of choler and melancholy.

ofte:	often
of:	from
fume:	vapour arising from the stomach
complecciouns:	an individual's temperament resulting from the mixture of the four humours
humours:	humours or bodily fluids
habundant:	excessive
wight:	person
met:	dreamt
cometh:	results
greete:	great
superfluytee:	excess
colera:	red bile, an excess of which produces a quick-tempered, vindictive, lustful temperament
causeth:	causes
dreden:	to be very afraid
arwes:	arrows
fyr:	fire
lemes:	flames
hem:	them
contek:	bloody strife
whelpes:	dogs
lyte:	small
malencolie:	black bile, an excess of which produces a frightened, quick-tempered individual lacking sound judgement
crie:	shout out
beres:	bears
boles:	bulls
develes:	devils
line 2938:	'that cause many a man such distress in sleep'
passe:	pass on
Catoun:	Dionysius Cato, to whom an elementary schoolbook of moral sayings was attributed
'Ne do no fors of dremes':	take no notice of dreams
flee:	fly
fro:	from
bemes:	perches
Goddes:	God's
as taak:	take
laxatyf:	laxative
up:	on
soule:	soul

conseille:	advise
the beste:	what is best
yow:	yourself
for:	so that
tarie:	waste time
toun:	town
apothecarie:	chemist
herbes:	herbs
techen:	direct
shul:	shall
been for youre hele:	make you better
prow:	benefit
tho:	those
fynde:	find
propretee:	special quality
by kynde:	naturally; 'which have naturally from their special virtue [the power]'(Sisam)
bynethe:	beneath, downwards
above:	upwards
foryet:	forget
owene:	own
coleryk:	choleric
ware:	beware (that)
ascencioun:	elevation, increasing altitude
repleet:	full
hoote:	hot
dar:	dare
leye:	bet
grote:	groat, silver coin
fevere terciane:	a fever which worsens every other day
agu:	ague, acute fever
bane:	death
digestyves:	things to aid digestion
wormes:	worms; a preparation of worms would be most suitable for a bird but it was also suggested for humans in medieval medicine. In the succeeding lines Pertelote suggests certain plants which will act as purges. There is disagreement amongst critics as to whether Pertelote is accurate in her recommendations or not
lawriol:	spurge laurel
centaure:	lesser centaury

fumetere: fumitory
ellebor: hellebore
groweth: grows
katapuce: caper spurge
gaitrys beryis: berries of the buckthorn
herbe yve: buck's-horn plantain
ther mery is: where it is pleasant
pekke: peck
for youre fader kyn: for the sake of your father's family

Lines 2970–3185

Chauntecleer's pride is hurt by the reduction of his nightmare to a mere physical disorder. He ironically thanks Pertelote for her erudition but he dismisses her evidence from Cato, saying that wiser men than Cato have believed that dreams are intimations of future joy or sorrow. He attempts to prove his case by quoting at length from a range of stories about dreams which have foretold events accurately. He begins with two tales from a classical source, either by the Latin author Cicero (106–43BC) or by the first-century Latin author Valerius Maximus. The first is of two men travelling on a pilgrimage who are forced to seek separate lodgings in a crowded town. One dreams that the other appeals to him to help prevent his murder. Although frightened by the dream the dreamer ignores it, even when he dreams the same event again. In the third appearance of his friend in a dream, the dreamer hears his friend's ghost relate that he has been murdered and his body hidden in a dung cart which will leave the city in the early morning. He claims that he has been murdered for his gold. In the morning the man is told that his friend has left the inn. Becoming suspicious and remembering his dream, he goes to the city gate and finds the dung cart. He calls out that his companion has been murdered and the people empty the cart to reveal the body of the murdered man. The moral drawn from the story is that murder cannot be concealed and the story ends with the carter and the innkeeper being hanged.

The second story also concerns two men on a journey. Prevented from immediately boarding a ship they wait and the contrary winds change so that they go to bed confident of sailing the next morning. However, one of the travellers dreams that a man warns him that he will be drowned if he sails on the following day. On waking he tells his friend of the dream but the friend refuses to accept the warning as he believes that dreams have no significance. Leaving his companion he embarks but, as the dream foretold, the boat is damaged and all perish. Chauntecleer stresses to Pertelote the necessity of heeding dreams as shown by these two stories.

For his third example Chauntecleer chooses the pathetic story of an early English saint, St Kenelm, who was murdered by a relative for his crown. Although warned by a dream interpreted for him by his nurse, the seven-year-old boy pays no heed because of his innocence and sanctity.

Chauntecleer then draws Pertelote's attention to the opinion of Macrobius on dreams and to the experiences of Daniel and Joseph as recounted in the Old Testament of the Bible. He also adds examples taken from the legends of ancient Greece. In conclusion, having stated his case learnedly and at length, Chauntecleer asserts that he is convinced of the danger that is in store for him. He will not take his wife's advice on laxatives as he does not like them and will not take them.

Having regained his authoritative position Chauntecleer flatters Pertelote. He mistranslates a Latin tag as a flattering reference to women and is willing to defy all dreams for his happiness with Pertelote. Having regained his good humour and confidence Chauntecleer parades up and down his yard escorted by his hens and mates many times with Pertelote in an exuberance of high spirits.

NOTES AND GLOSSARY

graunt mercy:	many thanks (polite usage)
of:	for
loore:	wisdom
natheless:	nonetheless
as touchyng:	regarding
renoun:	reputation
bad:	said
no dremes for to drede:	that no dreams were to be feared
olde:	old
bookes:	books
rede:	read
moore of auctorite:	of greater authority
evere:	ever
thee:	thrive
al the revers:	the exact opposite
sentence:	opinion
founden:	found
significaciouns:	signs
tribulaciouns:	troubles

enduren:	endure
argument:	formal proof
verray:	actual
preeve:	test of experience
sheweth:	shows
in dede:	in practice
oon:	one
gretteste:	greatest
auctour:	author: translate as authors
felawes:	friends
wente:	went
pilgrimage:	pilgrimage, a journey to a holy place or saint's shrine
in a ful good entente:	with good purpose
happed:	it occurred
coomen:	came
congregacioun:	a crowd
peple:	people
streit:	short
herbergage:	accommodation
founde:	found
ylogged:	lodged
of necessitee:	through necessity
departen:	part
gooth:	goes
hostelrye:	inn
loggyng:	lodging
as it wolde falle:	as it happened
stalle:	shed
fer:	far off
that oother:	the other
aventure:	luck
governeth:	governs
in commune:	univèrsally
mordered:	murdered
ther:	where
lye:	lie
abrayde:	started up
keep:	notice
thoughte:	seemed
twies:	twice
dremed:	dreamt

atte:	at the
thridde:	third
yet:	yet again
slawe:	slain
bihoold:	see (imperative)
woundes:	wounds
arys up:	get up (imperative)
erly:	early
in the morwe tyde:	in the morning
carte:	cart
dong:	dung
shaltow:	you will (shalt thou)
se:	see
prively:	secretly
thilke:	that same
do . . . arresten:	have . . . stopped
mordre:	murder
point:	detail
hewe:	colour
truste:	believe (imperative)
foond:	found
soone:	soon
in:	inn
after:	for
hostiler:	landlord
is agon:	has departed
fallen:	became
in suspecioun:	suspicious
remembrynge on:	remembering
lenger:	longer
lette:	delay
wente:	going
as it were:	as if
to donge:	to spread dung
lond:	on the land
arrayed:	arranged
wise:	way
devyse:	describe
hardy:	bold
felonye:	crime
lith gapyng upright:	lies on his back open-mouthed
ministres:	officers of the law

kepe:	watch over
reulen:	rule
citee:	city
harrow!:	help!
heere:	here
line 3046:	'Why should I add anything further to this story?' (Coghill and Tolkien)
sterte:	rushed
caste:	threw
to grounde:	to the ground
myddel:	middle
al newe:	recently
blisful:	holy
art:	are
trewe:	true
biwreyest:	reveal
alway:	always
Mordre wol out:	murder will out, will come out
wlatsom:	loathsome
abhomynable:	unnatural
resonable:	equitable
suffre:	allow
heled:	concealed
abyde:	waits
yeer:	year
hent:	seized
pyned:	tortured
engyued	tortured
biknewe:	confessed
wikkednesse:	evil
anhanged:	hanged
nekke-bon:	neck
heere:	in this way
to drede:	to be feared
nexte:	next
chapitre:	chapter
gabbe:	lie
blis:	happiness
see:	sea
certeyn cause:	a certain reason
contree:	country
if that:	if

contrarie:	adverse
tarie:	wait
haven-syde:	the side of a harbour
agayn:	towards
even-tyde:	evening
chaunge:	to change
hem leste:	they wished
jolif:	cheerful
reste:	rest
casten hem:	resolved
saille:	sail
o:	one
fil:	happened
mervaille:	marvel
hym mette:	he dreamt
wonder:	strange
beddes:	bed's
comanded:	ordered
abyde:	wait
tomorwe:	tomorrow
wende:	go
dreynt:	drowned
at an ende:	finished
wook:	woke
preyde:	begged
viage:	journey
lette:	postpone
scorned him ful faste:	'poured scorn upon him' (Sisam)
line 3089:	'that I will delay doing my business' (Sisam)
sette:	set
straw:	straw; straw being an object of small value
dremynges:	dreams
japes:	tricks
alday:	constantly
owles:	owls
maze:	delusive thing
therwithal:	as well
thyng:	a thing
shal:	shall be
sith:	since
forslewthen:	waste through laziness
wilfully:	deliberately

tyde:	time
it reweth me:	I'm sorry for it
leve:	leave
cours:	journey
yseyled:	sailed
myschaunce:	accident
eyled:	affected
casuelly:	by accident
shippes:	ship's
botme:	bottom
rente:	tore
othere:	other
seyled:	sailed
ensamples:	examples
maistow:	can you (mayst thou)
leere:	learn
to:	too
recchelees:	heedless
Seint Kenelm:	Saint Kenelm, an early English saint, reputed to have succeeded his father to the throne of the Mercian kingdom in 821 at the age of seven and to have been murdered on his aunt's instructions. An incident in the later legend was that before his death Kenelm dreamt that he climbed a tree which was cut down beneath him by his friends
Kenulphus:	Cenwulf, Kenelm's father
sone:	son
Mercenrike:	the kingdom of Mercia, one of the areas of Anglo-Saxon England
a lite:	a short time
avysioun:	vision
say:	saw
norice:	nurse
expowned:	explained
deel:	part
to kepe hym:	to guard himself
for:	against
traisoun:	treachery

litel tale hath he toold: 'he attached little importance to' (Sisam)

hooly: pure

I hadde levere than my sherte: 'I would hold it dearer than my shirt' (Coghill and Tolkein)

rad:	read
legende:	story
Macrobeus:	Macrobius, a scholar whose early fifth-century commentary on Cicero's *Somnium Scipionis* includes a discussion of types of dreams
Affrike:	Africa
worthy:	noble
Cipioun:	Scipio Africanus Minor, the conqueror of Carthage, who was shown his future triumph by his grandfather in a dream
affermeth:	confirms the truth of
after:	afterwards
forthermoore:	moreover
looketh:	consider
olde testament:	the Old Testament of the Bible
Daniel:	Daniel, a Jew, who interpreted the dream of Nebuchadnezzar and who himself had visions of the future of the Jews (see the Book of Daniel)
Joseph:	Joseph, a Jew, whose ability to interpret the Egyptian Pharaoh's dreams earned him wealth and position (see Genesis 40; 41)
Egipte:	Egypt
Pharao:	Pharaoh
bakere:	baker
butiller:	butler
wher:	whether
felte:	felt
noon effect:	no consequences of
whoso:	anyone who
seken:	seek
actes:	histories
sondry:	various
remes:	kingdoms
Cresus:	Croesus, king of Lydia, dreamt symbolically of his death, his dream being interpreted by his daughter
Lyde:	Lydia in Asia Minor
Andromacha:	Andromache, the wife of the Trojan hero, Hector; the dream is not in Homer's account but in a spurious Latin history
Ector:	Hector of Troy
sholde:	was to
lese:	loose

biforn:	before
lorn:	lost
bataille:	battle
availle:	avail
for to fighte:	to fight
Achilles:	Achilles, a Greek prince who slew Hector, according to Homer's *Iliad*
ny:	near
dwelle:	delay
as for conclusioun:	in conclusion
adversitee:	adversity
ne telle ... no stoor:	set no store by
venymous:	poisonous
diffye:	denounce
never a deel:	not at all
myrthe:	cheerful things
stynte:	stop
large:	bounteous
grace:	good fortune
beautee:	beauty
yen:	eyes
drede:	fear
for to dyen:	die away
siker:	sure
In principio:	'In the beginning', the opening words of the Gospel of St John in the New Testament in the Bible and also of Genesis in the Old Testament: 'as true as the Gospel'
Mulier est hominis confusio:	'Woman is man's downfall', a common clerical sentiment
sentence:	meaning
a-nyght:	at night
softe:	soft
al be it:	although
on yow ryde	mate with you
for that:	because
narwe:	narrow
solas:	delight
diffye:	reject
fley:	flew
beem:	beam
chuk:	noise made by poultry

corn:	grain of corn
lay in the yerd:	which was lying in the yard
real:	regal
namoore:	no longer
fethered:	covered with his feathers, mated with
trad:	trod, mated with
pryme:	prime was one of the Canonical hours at which prayers were said, it being the first at 6.00 a.m.: prime could also refer to the time 6.00 a.m.–9.00 a.m. or even to 9.00 a.m.
as it were:	like
leoun:	lion
rometh:	walks
hym deigned nat:	he did not deign
rennen:	run
roial:	regal
leve:	leave
pasture:	act of feeding
aventure:	adventure

Lines 3187–3214

Later in the day, the third of May, the main events occur. The date is fixed with accurate astronomical precision to indicate the significance of the day and Chauntecleer, who is endowed with similar knowledge, is able to identify the exact time of day. He is made happy by the spring and draws Pertelote's attention to the bird-song and flowers as indications of the season's pleasures which delight all true lovers. In a sudden change of mood Chauntecleer becomes sad. The narrator comments that all earthly happiness ends in sorrow, a truth universally acknowledged. He assures his audience that his tale of the cock is as true as the romance of Sir Lancelot of the Lake, so much liked by the ladies—as true that is as all fictional stories.

NOTES AND GLOSSARY

maked:	created; it was believed that God created the earth about the spring equinox, 21 March
compleet:	finished
thritty:	thirty; the date is 3 May as the 31 days of March, the 30 days of April and 2 days of May have gone since March began
dayes:	days

pryde:	self-esteem
caste up:	cast up
eÿen:	eyes
signe of Taurus:	the second sign of the Zodiac, Taurus the Bull
yronne:	run
degrees:	degrees; each sign has 30 degrees
kynde:	instinct
loore:	teaching
blisful:	joyful
stevene:	voice
is clomben:	has climbed
on:	in
hevene	the heavens
worldes blis:	happiness in the world
herkneth:	listen to
fresshe:	fresh
floures:	flowers
sprynge:	grow
revel:	merriment
sodeynly:	suddenly
hym:	to him
fil:	happened
sorweful:	sad
cas:	event
wo:	misery
soone:	soon
ago:	past
rethor:	great writer
faire:	well
endite:	write
cronycle:	history
saufly:	confidently
sovereyn:	supreme
notabilitee:	fact worth noting
herkne:	listen
storie:	story
also . . . as:	as . . . as
undertake:	swear
Launcelot de Lake:	Sir Lancelot of the Lake, a knight of King Arthur's Round Table, a chivalrous hero
that:	which/who (probably refers to Lancelot rather than the book)

reverence:	esteem
torne:	turn
sentence:	subject

Lines 3215–66

Turning again to the story, the narrator introduces the fox, the villain of the tale, who has broken into the yard during the night and is waiting to seize Chauntecleer, hiding in a clump of plants. The narrator, in a rhetorical style, curses the deceitful fox and the day on which the cock has left his perch despite the warning dream. This leads him to a brief discussion of the problem of man's freedom of action and the possible restriction placed upon human choice by God's foreknowledge of all events. Without coming to any conclusion and admitting that the discussion is inappropriate to the circumstances of the tale, the narrator returns to the farmyard. Yet, as before, the reference of the story has been enlarged by the introduction of a topic not associated with birds and this increases both the humour and the relevance of the tale to human behaviour.

Then the narrator blames Pertelote for Chauntecleer's misfortune as she has counselled him to ignore his dream. Indeed, all human misery is woman's fault as Eve was responsible for Adam's being expelled from the Garden of Eden. Conscious that he may displease some of the audience the narrator excuses himself by saying that it is all a joke and that other learned men may hold different opinions. Indeed, the views expressed are not those of the narrator but of the cock, Chauntecleer.

NOTES AND GLOSSARY

col-fox:	probably a fox with black markings
iniquitee:	wickedness
woned:	lived
yeres:	years
heigh:	exalted
ymaginacioun:	vision
forncast:	fore-ordained probably 'by divine foreknowledge' referring to God's eternal vision or possibly to Chauntecleer's dream
thurghout:	through
hegges:	hedges
brast:	burst
ther:	where
wont:	accustomed

repaire:	resort
wortes:	plants, probably vegetables
stille:	still
undren:	strictly 9.00 a.m., but could be applied to the morning between 9.00 and 12.00
waitynge:	watching for
tyme:	opportunity
gladly:	eagerly
homycides:	murderers
in await liggen:	lie in ambush
mordrour:	murderer
lurkynge:	lurking
newe:	new
Scariot:	Judas Iscariot, the disciple who betrayed Jesus Christ
Genylon:	Ganelon who, in the old French poem, *The Song of Roland*, betrayed the rearguard of Charlemagne's army at the battle of Roncesvalles
dissymulour:	deceiver
Greek Synon:	the Greek Sinon, who, after being captured by the Trojans, persuaded Priam to bring the wooden horse full of Greeks into Troy
broghtest:	brought
Troye:	the city of Troy
outrely:	utterly
morwe:	morning
flaugh:	flew
ywarned:	warned
forwoot:	has foreknowledge of
nedes:	necessarily. As Chauntecleer has ignored his dream and flown from the safety of the beam, the narrator introduces the discussion of whether man is free to choose his own course of action or whether God's foreknowledge of all events means that all actions are predetermined. This topic was one of great theological interest and often discussed, and here the briefly stated argument follows the distinctions and conclusions reached in Boethius's *Consolation of Philosophy*. The figure of Philosophy in her discussion with Boethius states that God can have foreknowledge and man free will. God exists in eternal time and all human past, present and future

is omnipresent to him. God can only know, not foreknow. Although God knows that a man will go for a walk, this does not oblige the man to walk. This necessity is called conditional as there is an element of human choice. Simple necessity is where there is no choice as, for example, that man must die or the sun must rise. Chaucer was much influenced by the thinking of Boethius and translated the *Consolation of Philosophy* (see p.96)

after:	according to
opinioun:	opinion
clerkis:	scholars
witnesse on:	take witness from
parfit:	perfect
in scole:	in the universities
altercacioun:	dispute
mateere:	subject
disputisoun:	debate
bulte:	sift the flour
bren:	husks: 'I cannot get to the bottom of this matter' (Coghill and Tolkien)
doctour:	teacher, doctor of the Church
Augustyn:	St Augustine of Hippo (354–430)
Boece:	a Roman consul, Boethius (*c.* 480–524) wrote the *Consolation of Philosophy*, a book very influential in the Middle Ages
Bisshop:	bishop, an official of the Church
Bradwardyn:	Thomas Bradwarding (*c.* 1290–1349), Archbishop of Canterbury and a writer
wheither:	whether
forwityng:	foreknowledge
streyneth:	constrains
nedely:	necessarily
clepe:	call
symple necessitee:	simple necessity
free choys:	free choice
graunted:	granted
wroght:	done
wityng:	knowledge
necessitee condicioneel:	conditional necessity
conseil:	advise
sorwe:	disastrous results

wommennes:	women's
ofte:	often
colde:	ruinous
wommannes:	a woman's
Adam:	the first man created by God
Paradys:	Paradise, the Garden of Eden
ther as:	where
wel at ese:	very comfortable
displese:	offend
passe over:	ignore it
for I seyde it in my game:	'for I was only joking' (Coghill and Tolkien)
trete of:	deal with
divyne:	suppose

Lines 3267–337

Chauntecleer, having regained his spirits, sings merrily and, watching a butterfly amongst the plants, he becomes aware of the fox. Although he does not want to cry out, Chauntecleer is so startled and alarmed that he crows and prepares to run away from an animal he instinctively recognises as his enemy. His flight is prevented by the reassuring words of the fox who calms Chauntecleer by denying that he intends to harm the cock. Indeed the only reason for his coming to the yard has been to hear Chauntecleer sing and he assures the cock of the fine quality of his voice. The fox has been acquainted with Chauntecleer's parents, especially with the musical performance of Chauntecleer's father in which, with both eyes closed and standing on tip-toe with his neck outstretched, he sang masterfully. In addition Chauntecleer's father was wise, wiser even than the cock in the story in *Daun Burnel the Asse*. He asks Chauntecleer to sing to see if he is as good as his father.

Chauntecleer is overcome by the fox's flattery and the narrator moralises, warning noble men of the dangers of flattery. The cock, unconcerned, copies his father's singing stance and is seized immediately by the fox and carried off to the wood on the fox's back.

NOTES AND GLOSSARY

faire:	elegantly
soond:	sand
hire:	herself
myrily:	with enjoyment
lith:	lies
agayn:	in

free:	noble
soong:	sang
mermayde:	mermaid; a mythical creature half woman, half fish
Phisiologus:	a bestiary, a book which combined zoological and moral descriptions of birds and animals
boterflye:	butterfly
war:	aware
ne liste hym:	he did not want
for to crowe:	to crow
cride:	cried out
sterte:	jumped
man:	one
affrayed:	frightened
natureelly:	by natural instinct
desireth:	wants
contrarie:	opposite
erst:	before
espye:	catch sight of
freend:	friend
feend:	fiend
vileynye:	injury
conseil:	secrets
oonly:	only
herkne:	hear
aungel:	angel
hevene:	heaven
therwith:	besides
musyk:	music
feelynge:	feeling
Boece:	Boethius also wrote a book on music, *De Musica*
fader:	father
soule:	soul
blesse:	bless
mooder:	mother
gentillesse:	courtesy
hous:	house
ybeen:	been
fayn:	gladly
plese:	please
for:	since
brouke:	enjoy (the use of)
save:	apart from

morwenynge: morning
of herte: from the heart
wolde so peyne hym: would exert himself
wynke: shut his eyes
loude: loudly
tiptoon: tip-toes
strecche: stretch
nekke: neck
smal: slender
discrecioun: good judgement
regioun: region
wisedom: wisdom
passe: surpass
Daun Burnel the Asse: a satirical poem *Speculum Stultorum* in which the adventures of an ass are described
vers: verses
for that: because
preestes: priest's
sone: son
yaf: gave
knok: blow
yong: young
nyce: foolish
for to lese: lose
benefice: church living
certeyn: certainly
nys: is not (ne is)
comparisoun: comparison
his: his, the cock in the story in *Speculum Stultorum*
subtiltee: cunning
seinte charitee: Saint Charity
countrefete: equal
wynges: wings
bete: beat
man: one
traysoun: treachery
ravysshed: entranced
flaterie: flattery
lordes: lords
flatour: flatterer
courtes: courts
losengeour: deceiver

plesen:	please
soothfastnesse:	the truth
redeth:	read
Ecclesiaste:	a reference to a biblical or apocryphal authority but critical opinion is divided
beth:	be
trecherye:	treachery
hye:	high
strecchynge:	stretching
heeld:	kept
cloos:	shut
for the nones:	for the occasion; often used to complete the metrical line rather than for its meaning
Russell:	'the red one'
atones:	at once
gargat:	throat
hente:	seized
bak:	back
beer:	bore
sewed:	chased

Lines 3338–74

The narrator, in mock-heroic style, laments the fate of Chauntecleer, which occurs on a Friday, the week-day dedicated to Venus, the goddess of love. He upbraids Venus for allowing her devoted servant to be caught in such a manner. Invoking the rhetorician Geoffrey de Vinsauf, the narrator is distressed that he lacks Geoffrey's skill in the composing of fitting laments for Chauntecleer.

The distress of Chauntecleer is mourned by Pertelote and the other hens, whose expressions of grief surpass those made for the great human tragedies occurring at the overthrow of Troy, Carthage and Rome. In particular Pertelote shrieks more vigorously than her human counterparts.

NOTES AND GLOSSARY

destinee:	destiny
eschewed:	evaded
roghte:	took notice
meschaunce:	ill-luck
Venus:	the Roman goddess of love
goddesse:	goddess

al his poweer:	all in his power
delit:	delight
world to multiplye:	to make populous the world
woldestow:	would you (woldest thou)
Gaufred:	Geoffrey de Vinsauf, whose book on rhetoric, *Nova Poetria*, was written at the end of the twelfth century
maister:	master
Richard:	Richard I, King of England (1189–99)
with shot:	by the shooting of an arrow
compleynedest:	lamented
deeth:	death
sentence:	noble sentiments
Friday:	Richard I was mortally wounded on Friday, 26 March 1199
shewe:	show
pleyne:	lament
peyne:	pain
lamentacion:	lamentation
Ylion:	Troy
wonne:	captured
Pirrus:	Pyrrhus slew the King of Troy, Priam
streite swerd:	drawn sword
hent:	seized
Eneydos:	the *Æneid* of Virgil (70–19BC)
clos:	enclosure
sighte:	sight
sovereynly:	above all others
shrighte:	shrieked
Hasdrubales:	Hasdrubal, leader of the Carthaginians, when Carthage was captured by the Romans in 146BC
Romayns:	Romans
brend:	burnt
Cartage:	Carthage
fyr:	fire
sterte:	leapt
stedefast:	steadfast
woful:	unhappy
Nero:	Nero, Emperor of Rome (AD54–68)
senatoures:	senators'
losten:	lost
withouten:	without
gilt:	guilt

Lines 3375-438

Hearing the noise of the hens, the widow and her daughters come outside and see the fox with the cock. Immediately they shout and start to chase the fox, joined by all the animals and neighbours, shouting and making noises on musical instruments. Suddenly Chauntecleer's fortunes change and addressing Russell he advises the fox to tell the people that their efforts are in vain as he, Russell, means to keep the cock. The fox, who cannot resist this appeal to his vanity in out-witting the humans, replies. Immediately he opens his mouth Chauntecleer flies to the safety of the nearest tree and, despite the gentle words of Russell that the cock has misinterpreted his intentions, Chauntecleer refuses to come down. He has learnt his lesson about succumbing to flattering and deceitful words and will in future keep his eyes open and be alert to such tricks. Russell sadly admits his fault, that of talking when he should have kept his mouth closed. Both have been flattered into their silly behaviour and both learn their lesson, a lesson emphasised by the narrator.

NOTES AND GLOSSARY

sely:	humble
out at dores:	out of the house
stirten:	rushed
syen:	saw
weylaway:	alas
staves:	sticks
dogge:	dog
dystaf:	distaff, used to wind wool in spinning
hogges:	hogs
fered:	frightened
berkyng:	barking
ronne:	ran
breeke:	broke
yolleden:	yelled
helle:	hell
dokes:	ducks
quelle:	to kill
gees:	geese
flowen:	flew
hydous:	hideous
benedicitee!:	bless us!
meynee:	crowd

shoutes: shouts

Jakke Straw: Jack Straw, one of the leaders of the Peasants' Revolt which occurred in southern England in 1381. They marched on London to make their demands known to the King and much rioting took place. Straw was caught and beheaded

shrille: shrill

Flemyng: the Flemings, prosperous foreign tradesmen, were brutally killed by the mob of peasants and Londoners, jealous of the Flemings' wealth

kille: to kill

bras: brass

bemes: trumpets

box: boxwood

boon: bone

blewe: blew

powped: tooted

skriked: shrieked

howped: whooped

semed: seemed

wys: surely

turneth agayn: turn back

proude: proud

cherles: peasants

pestilence: plague

maugree youre heed: in spite of your head; despite all you can do

brak: broke

delyverly: deftly

ydoon: done

trespas: wrong

in as muche as: in so far as

wikke: evil

entente: purpose

mente: meant

shrewe: curse

bothe: both

bigyle: beguile

ofter: more often

ones: once

do: cause

thee: thrive

God yeve: God give

undiscreet:	lacking in judgment
governaunce:	self-control
jangleth:	chatters
holde his pees:	keep silent
recchelees:	thoughtless
necligent:	negligent
truste on:	believe in

Lines 3438–46

The narrator ends his tale by requesting his audience not to dismiss the story simply as the adventures of a cock, a fox and a hen. All writings can have moral significance and he asks that his tale be understood as he has intended it to be, with a more profound meaning than a mere animal fable. He ends suitably with a prayer to God.

NOTES AND GLOSSARY

holden:	consider
folye:	silly thing
taketh:	understand
moralite:	moral (of the tale)
seint Peul:	Saint Paul, an early convert to Christianity whose writings form much of the New Testament of the Bible
to our doctrine:	for our instruction
ywrite:	written: see The Letter of Paul to the Romans, 15:4
lat the chaf be stille:	leave the husks alone (Coghill and Tolkien)
as seith my lord:	critics do not know to whom or what this refers
Amen:	amen, the formal end of a prayer

Lines 3447–62

This epilogue is found in some manuscripts and there has been critical dispute as to whether it is genuine. It seems probable that Chaucer did write it but subsequently cancelled it. In it the Host praises the Nun's Priest for his tale in terms which reflect the Host's interest in manliness rather than in morality.

NOTES AND GLOSSARY

i-blessed:	blessed
breche:	breeches
stoon:	testicle

seculer:	a layman, not a cleric
trede-foul:	male bird
aright:	all right
corage:	desire
nede:	in need
wene:	think
moo:	more
seventene:	seventeen
whiche:	what
braunes:	muscles
breest:	chest
sperhauk:	sparrow-hawk, a hawk which catches small birds known as sparrows
colour:	complexion
dyen:	dye
brasile:	a red dye
greyn of Portyngale:	grain of Portugal, a red dye
faire falle your:	good luck to you (Coghill and Tolkien)
chere:	behaviour

Part 3

Commentary

Source material

On a first reading *The Nun's Priest's Tale* may appear as a narrative 'of a fox, or of a cok and hen', as a story of talking birds and beasts. Yet the tale is enriched and our enjoyment increased if we can appreciate that the author's treatment of his plot, his use of style, vocabulary, structure and characterisation contribute to the effect of the story. It is the purpose of this part to discuss the ways in which Chaucer develops the familiar animal fable to meet his own artistic requirements.

The genre to which this tale belongs is that of the animal fable, which is 'a short story devised to convey some useful lesson; *especially* one in which animals or inanimate things are the speakers or actors' (*Oxford English Dictionary*). The animals are given the physical and moral attributes of men and women and the reader is expected to learn a lesson from the words and actions of the characters which he can apply to his own behaviour. Often the lesson is a simple one, as apparently in *The Nun's Priest's Tale*: the reader learns from Chauntecleer's behaviour to be alert, to be on one's guard especially against flatterers and, from Russell's behaviour, the reader learns the value of keeping one's mouth closed and of remaining silent. Authors have used, and still use, the animal fable to convey a moral or political message for, by using animals, it is the reader who must make the connection with human life which the author has left deliberately unstated. It is a safe way to convey unpopular moral or dangerous political statements but also it can be a sophisticated method of teaching. As human beings we laugh readily at many of the absurdities of animals and birds and it is only later that we realise rather soberly that the lesson also applies to ourselves.

Of ancient origins, the animal fable had been a popular form of entertainment so that Chaucer was using a narrative form which would have been familiar to his audience. In his own earlier works, *The House of Fame* and *The Parliament of Fowls,* Chaucer had used talking birds as characters in these dream poems and in *The Squire's Tale* and *The Manciple's Tale,* both Canterbury Tales, talking birds appear again. In *The Nun's Priest's Tale* Chaucer is careful to preserve the framework of the animal fable and to make his tale work as such. The birds and animals are the major characters and this is stressed by their being given names, whilst the human actors remain anonymous. The action of the tale is concerned with the lives of Chauntecleer, Pertelote, and Russell, and the human beings have no significant role in the plot. Throughout the tale Chaucer is consistent in his presentation of the birds and animals as birds and animals. With one major difference, Chauntecleer and Pertelote are birds. They live in a farmyard, roost on a beam in a coop, eat corn, crow, cluck, walk about and mate frequently. Similarly, Russell is a fox in all his actions. He lurks in the vegetable plot, is the enemy of the poultry and, at the first opportunity, seizes Chauntecleer and runs off with him. Chaucer maintains his tale as an animal fable and, in common with the genre, the exception to normal animal behaviour is the capacity of the animals and birds to talk to each other in human speech. It is because Chaucer is consistent in his presentation of their animal and avian behaviour that we are able to accept, on one level, the simple morals of the tale at the end. Yet this is only one element of *The Nun's Priest's Tale* for in style, structure and characterisation Chaucer elaborates the basic animal fable to make it something other than a simple fable. Although it works and has a meaning as an animal fable, through a consideration of Chaucer's stylistic treatment of the tale a more complex and interesting work emerges. This elaboration can be appreciated more easily if the previous forms of the tale are considered.

Whilst no direct source for Chaucer's tale has been identified it is clear that both the plot and the characters owe much to earlier stories of the cock and the fox. Although the most influential work on *The Nun's Priest's Tale* appears to be a twelfth-century poem, *Le Roman de Renard,* the animal fable has classical origins, the earliest being ascribed to Aesop, a Greek of the sixth century BC. Through adaptation and expansion, various Latin translations and use as a school text book, these tales were transmitted during the early Middle Ages and in them can be recognised the tricks which Chaucer uses in his tale. Flattering references to singing and voices result in welcome gifts or escapes from dangerous situations and the combination of the two tricks and morals used by Chaucer has an early form in an eleventh-century story of a fox and a partridge. The coupling of the fox and cock with references to parental abilities and the tricks appear in two twelfth-century poems, the Latin poem *Gallus and Vulpes,* and the French collection of fables, *Ysopet*, written by Marie de France in England. Whilst the tricks, morals and some elaboration of the basic plot had developed by this time, it is the cycle of French poems *Le Roman de Renard* which enriched the basic elements into new creations and inspired imitations throughout Europe.

The earliest part of the cycle of stories which makes up *Le Roman de Renard* was written by a Frenchman, Pierre de Saint Cloud, about 1175 and is concerned with the enmity between the fox, Renard, and the wolf, Isengrim. The author, basing his stories on earlier literature, created amusing tales which prompted later authors to add further adventures of Renard. Thus *Le Roman de Renard* is a collection of stories composed between 1175 and 1250 and made up of a number of branches, each branch containing one or more stories. Other French poems were written later in the thirteenth century but in these poems the animal characters were used for purposes of satire, political criticism and didactic instruction. Instead of giving pleasure, the stories became moral allegories and Renard the fox a symbol of evil and hypocrisy, often representing the devil.

The popularity of stories also inspired foreign authors, the earliest extant version being the German poem, *Reinhart Fuchs*, by Heinrich der Glîchesaere written about 1190. Based mainly on the earlier branches, the tale of Renard and Chauntecler* is included. A thirteenth-century Flemish poem, *Reinaert de Vos*, became very popular and influential. Also in the same century an Italian poem, *Rainardo e Lesengrino*, was written. In England there appears to be only one poem, *Of the Vox and of the Wolf*, written about 1250, which precedes Chaucer's story. However, it does seem that the adventures of Renard were known in England, although not recorded in a permanent literary form. Evidence from wood carvings and manuscript illuminations suggests an oral transmission of the tales. Interest in animals is confirmed by the bestiaries, books in which the behaviour and characteristics of animals and birds were illustrated often with a moral and religious significance. In *The Nun's Priest's Tale* Chaucer refers to such a book *Physiologus*, at lines 3271 and 3272, and such material was used in sermons and other medieval literature.

Critics seem agreed that Chaucer's probable source for his poem was a version of the story of Renard and Chauntecler as told in *Le Roman de Renard* but not the exact French version which we have today. Similarities noticed between Chaucer's tale and the German poem, *Reinhart Fuchs*, possibly come from a common source but no firm conclusion as to source material can be made. However, in Pierre de Saint Cloud's account of the tale of the fox and the cock which occurs at the beginning of his poem many features, which are present in Chaucer's rendering, can be seen.

*Note the different spelling in the original.

The following outline gives the main features of the plot:

(*i*) Renard the fox, who is the main character, visits the rich farm of Constant des Noes. Although the yard is fenced, Renard finds a broken paling, creeps in and hides in the cabbage plot. He is seen by the hens who run away.

(*ii*) Chauntecler, aroused by the noise, asks his favourite hen, Pinte, what has happened. Pinte admits to being frightened by a wild beast and refuses to be comforted by the cock. However, Chauntecler declares the animal to be an illusion and settles down for a rest.

(*iii*) Tired, Chauntecler sleeps and dreams of a beast with a red coat with a collar of bone, which the beast forces on Chauntecler, who is terrified by the tightness of the collar. Frightened, Chauntecler rushes to Pinte, who upraids Chauntecler for being a coward and tells him not to scare the hens. Chauntecler reports his dream and asks Pinte for an interpretation. Pinte warns him that the animal is the fox, the bone is his teeth and the collar his mouth, and that he is waiting for Chauntecler amongst the cabbages. Chauntecler dismisses Pinte's warning and refuses to believe the message of the dream.

(*iv*) Chauntecler dozes and Renard approaches, jumps but misses Chauntecler, who leaps on a dunghill. Renard reassures Chauntecler that he is the cock's cousin and reminisces about the singing prowess of Chauntecler's father, who crew with closed eyes. Chauntecler is suspicious, so Renard protests his innocence, but Chauntecler will only sing if the fox retreats. Still perturbed, Chauntecler crows with one eye open. Renard is contemptuous of Chauntecler's feeble attempt, so, shutting both eyes, Chauntecler crows again. Immediately he is seized by Renard. Seeing what has happened, Pinte laments her lord's fate and her own.

(*v*) The hue and cry is raised and the chase ensues.

(*vi*) Chauntecler draws Renard's attention to the insults of the pursuers and tempts him to shout back. Renard does so and Chauntecler escapes to a tree. Triumphantly Chauntecler mocks Renard's folly and the fox curses the mouth which should remain closed. Chauntecler curses the eyes which should remain open and sends Renard on his way.

Whilst it is clear that Chaucer inherited much of his material, it is his adaptations and additions which create a new and unique version of a traditional story. Even though the elements of Chaucer's tale are present in the version from the *Renard* cycle, it is Chaucer's arrangement and expansion of these elements which produce *The Nun's Priest's Tale*. Chaucer's first adaptation is visible in the construction of the story, for although the encounter between Chauntecleer and Russell is for many readers the most vivid, comic and memorable incident in the poem, this meeting does not occur until approximately two thirds of the way through the poem. Unlike earlier versions, the greater part of the tale is concerned not with action but with discussion, with apparently learned debates on dreams, ill health and medicines between two birds who believe in talking things over in true matrimonial fashion. Chaucer appears to be more interested in what his characters say rather than in what they do, to be more concerned with the presentation of ideas than with the presentation of actions. Thus the tricks which produce the action, that of Russell to make Chauntecleer sing with closed eyes and that of Chauntecleer to make the fox open his mouth, are developed in the last part of the tale. In the major section Chaucer, using the idea in the *Renard* cycle, expands the discussion on dreams, their causes and interpretations, within the context of a matrimonial disagreement. In this way Chaucer can present a topic which concerned him deeply and which is reflected in the many discussions of it in his poetry, whilst at the same time developing the characters of the birds through the content and manner of their discussion. This deliberately slow pace and the postponement of the action appear in other works by Chaucer and reflect both his own interest in discussion and its use as a method of revealing character, and the circumstances of composition. Chaucer, by using known material, would be addressing an audience already familiar with the plot of the story. His audience would be interested not in what happened, for that they knew, but how it happened, in what ways the author made the known events plausible and convincing. In *The Nun's Priest's Tale* Chaucer relegates the traditional action of the fable to the last third of his poem, whilst two thirds are spent on portraying the characters of Chauntecleer and Pertelote through their own discussions. In this way Chaucer tantalises his audience and makes them wait for the expected tricks and chase, which appear all the more brilliant and exciting in contrast with the lengthy and almost tedious discussion of the birds. This shift of emphasis is reflected in the headings given to the tale by scribes in the existing manuscripts. The majority of the complete or practically complete manuscripts of *The Canterbury Tales* have no specific heading, but of those that do twelve of the sixteen refer to the cock and hen. The heading in the Ellesmere manuscript reads 'Heere bigynneth the Nonnes Preestes Tale of the Cok and Hen, Chauntecleer and Pertelote' with no mention of the fox, Russell.

Having discussed in general the alteration which Chaucer made in the arrangement of his material a more detailed examination of the plot will make this clear. It will also help to assess the nature of the additional material which will be discussed in the following section.

Chaucer's elaboration of the basic plot is shown by two main developments: firstly, the elaboration of the personalities given to the cock and the hen; secondly, the comments made by the narrator which are important stylistically. Chaucer's interest in human motivation and character, portrayed through the medium of the birds, is reflected in the extra material added to the plot. After Chauntecleer's frightened account of his dream, Pertelote upraids her husband for his cowardly behaviour and gives the qualities which she thinks make the ideal husband. Her practical nature is demonstrated through her attribution of Chauntecleer's dream to a bodily disorder. Displaying her knowledge of the physical causes of dreams, she can recommend the remedy which Chauntecleer must take to recover from these disturbing dreams. Thus, Chaucer includes references to the medieval concepts of the humours and medicinal remedies. Similarly with Chauntecleer, Chaucer, in demonstrating his character, allows the cock to argue about the validity of the prophetic nature of dreams by reference to a list of stories in which dreams foretold the future. We understand the pompous, self-assured bird through the pretentious accounts of the classical tragedies and biblical stories. None of the material given to the bird is necessary to the action of the plot. It is necessary to what the narrator wishes to demonstrate about human nature.

After the long, human discussion the narrator reduces Chauntecleer and Pertelote to poultry again. Lines 3172–86 re-establish Chauntecleer as a cock, behaving as a bird, although an extraordinary cock whose demeanour makes him lion-like and whose pride is evident in every action.

In the second part of the tale it is Chauntecleer's behaviour as a bird which is stressed. The elaboration of this later part comes, not so much through character presentation, but through comments made by the narrator on the action. A generalising comment by the narrator on sorrow and joy and authorial truth (3205–14) follows Chauntecleer's sudden change of mood. Similarly, after the introduction of Russell, the narrator comments upon the nature of traitors (3226–9), curses the day on which Chauntecleer ignores the warning of his dream (3230–3), muses upon the predestination of human actions (3234–50) and warns of the danger of accepting female advice (3251–5). Lines 3325–30 comment upon the danger of flattery just as Chauntecleer is about to succumb to the fox's pleasing words, and after his capture the narrator addresses Destiny (3338–41), Venus (3342–6) and a famous rhetorician, Geoffrey de Vinsauf (3347–54). The shrieking hens are likened to the lamenting women in several classical stories (3355–73) and there is a reference to Fortune at lines 3403 and 3404. At the end of the tale the narrator directs the audience's minds to the consideration of the true meaning of the story by suggesting that it is something more than a mere account of the actions of a hen and a cock and a fox.

It can be seen that Chaucer adapts an existing story to suit his own purposes. As the story is to say something about human nature, Chaucer chooses to elaborate the personalities of the cock and hen. This necessitates the inclusion of material which, although connected with the tale, does not advance the action but develops the two main characters. This personality elaboration means that the main action of the plot is delayed to the final section, thus achieving a startling and vivid end. The narratorial comments help to delay the action further and increase the tension but, more importantly, they provide the tone for the second part of the tale. We are shown that Chauntecleer's behaviour does lead him into trouble, that he escapes death by a hair's breadth and that the tale almost becomes a tragedy. It is not a tragedy for Chauntecleer saves himself, but not until the last moment. Neither can it be a tragedy when considered only as the story of a cock and a fox, but the style of the narrator's comments and the tone they create has a relevance to the human implications of the story.

Characterisation and content

In the preceding section we have seen how Chaucer elaborated the basic plot by the addition of material which delays the central action of the existing fable until the end of *The Nun's Priest's Tale*. The elaboration can be seen, firstly, in the characterisation of the main participants and, secondly, in the styles in which Chaucer tells his tale.

The manner in which Chaucer elaborates the characters of the cock and hen reflect his own interest in human nature and human relationships, as well as various intellectual ideas which fascinated him. As a poet Chaucer was concerned throughout his work with the many and various forms of human love and desire. In a number of *The Canterbury Tales* the relationship of marriage, with or without love, is of central importance and especially the question of who should be the dominant partner. Similarly the notion of dreams, their causes and significance had preoccupied Chaucer in his earlier poetry, as had the philosophical problem of whether man's actions on earth were predestined or whether man had free will. All three of these concerns can be recognised in many of Chaucer's works but in *The Nun's Priest's Tale* they are brought together for a comic purpose, although with more serious implications.

In his desire to explore character through the presentation of certain ideas, Chaucer exploited the conventions of the animal fable. As the fable is used to convey a lesson applicable to human moral behaviour, the animals and birds often behave in a quasi-human fashion, displaying virtues and vices appropriate to human action but absent from the non-moral world of beasts. As we accept that animals talk in such stories so too we accept other aspects of human behaviour. In *The Nun's Priest's Tale* Chaucer, with great imagination, establishes the relationship of marriage between Chauntecleer and Pertelote. The relationship, absurd in a bird sense, is a basic human situation, which Chaucer can exploit knowing it to be familiar to his audience. The disagreement between the birds arises partly from the different personalities but also from the peculiar tensions of domestic happiness. By making the dispute the product of such a plausible situation Chaucer makes the application of the birds' behaviour to human circumstances easier. The tale works brilliantly on several levels. As an animal fable, the story cannot stray too far from behaviour applicable to birds; on the moral level, the behaviour must be suitable for human significance and as a story, the plot must have its hero, heroine and villain. It is in the interweaving and maintaining of these strands that much of the brilliance and subtlety of *The Nun's Priest's Tale* lies.

The two characters through whom Chaucer develops his ideas and thus their personalities are Chauntecleer and Pertelote, the cock being 'on stage' throughout the tale. Chauntecleer is presented both through his own actions and words and through descriptions of his appearance and behaviour. The first of these descriptions follows that of the poor widow at the start of the tale when the narrator presents the hero of his tale – and there is no doubt that Chauntecleer is the hero. In contrast with the drab and sombre description of the widow and her sober responsible behaviour, Chauntecleer glitters and flashes. In contrast with the restraint and strained circumstances of human beings, the yard, with its surrounding fence and ditch, is governed by a superlative cock. Instead of the negatives used in the description of the widow, the narrator uses comparatives all of which are in Chauntecleer's favour. The hero, the first male creature mentioned in the story, is named and described in great detail. Firstly in his presentation, the narrator draws attention to Chauntecleer's crowing, the regularity of which based on

Chauntecleer's instinctive knowledge of astronomy, enables human beings to tell the time. The cock's utility links him with the other animals mentioned earlier in the tale, but, by emphasising the cock's crowing by placing it first in the description, the impression is conveyed that this is what Chauntecleer himself considers his most notable attribute. As we realise later the pride in his song is the way to his humiliation, for the fox, through flattery, is able to exploit this pride.

Through the colourful description of Chauntecleer both his appearance and his character are conveyed. The narrator, in correct rhetorical fashion, describes the cock from his head to his toes, all the similes he uses conveying the idea of something precious and rare. 'Fyn coral' and 'jeet' are not only of a beautiful colour but are used as jewelry. The colours red, black, azure, white and gold suggest the brilliance of an heraldic design on a shield or flag and this military association is reinforced by likening Chauntecleer's comb to a castle wall. Thus the narrator, through his use of vocabulary and imagery, suggests the noble, proud bearing of his hero, the cock, yet links the description with human associations.

This combination of human and avian is continued in the nobility of bearing, associated with lords and ladies, attributed to Chauntecleer. Chauntecleer is a 'gentil cok', that is, a cock of noble breeding who behaves courteously and with consideration towards the hens whom he controls. These hens are 'his sustres and his paramours', that is both offspring of the same parents and his lovers. In this one line we can see the narrator's skill in combining both the avain and human characteristics of Chauntecleer. As a cock he may well be produced from the same clutch of eggs as his hens and as poultry it does not matter whether he mates with his sisters, but, by the introduction of the human concept of love, the narrator makes a joke about the indiscriminate behavour of chickens and the impropriety of such behaviour amongst people. What may occur in the farmyard is not suitable in the hall. 'Gentil', 'governaunce', 'plesaunce', 'paramours', all these words suggest the gracious behaviour of lords and ladies as does the form of address, 'faire damoysele'. Here the narrator is using a style, to be discussed more fully later, in which he describes inferior beings, cocks and hens, by a style more suited to superior beings, lords and ladies. In one way this is correct. Stories are normally about superior people described in this fashion, so it is correct that this hero and heroine should be described in this way, but this hero and heroine are poultry and therefore it is a joke to present them thus.

The narrator proceeds from the general to the particular, from the hens to the special favourite, Pertelote, and describes the relationship between his hero and heroine in terms appropriate to courtly lovers. Since her youth Pertelote's behaviour has been so ladylike that she had enslaved the heart of Chauntecleer and they live together in the harmony of perfect happiness singing love duets. As the description of the poultry has opened with a reference to song so it ends with one. Yet the two references are very different and demonstrate the skill with which the conventions of the fable have been used. The first reference is to crowing, an acceptable occupation for a cock: the second reference is to the singing of love duets, an absurdity between birds. Yet we accept the absurdity and the explanation of the narrator at lines 2880 and 2881 because of the brilliant mixture of human and bird characteristics used throughout the description. The demands of the story, of the fable and of the application to human behaviour have all been maintained with great skill.

This opening description establishes the setting for the subsequent discussion between the hero and heroine on the human concern of dreams and their meanings. For this reason the birds' human characteristics are established in this first description. A second account, lines 3172 to 3186, which occurs after the dispute, stresses Chauntecleer's behaviour as a bird and from these descriptions, although a literary hero has been established, the accuracy of the physical appearance is such to have led one critic, Lalia P. Boone, to recognise the type of poultry described.* John M. Steadman, in an article in *Isis* in 1959, demonstrated that the characters of Chauntecleer and Pertelote were based on the lore of medieval natural history. Referring to the late fourteenth-century English translation made by John of Trevisa of *De Proprietatibus Rerum* by Bartholomaeus Anglicus, Steadman showed that the characteristics of the lover, the warrior and the songster were attributed to a cock. As a lover, the cock finds food for his wives and gives them preference, a characteristic noted in the tale at lines 3174 to 3175 and at lines 3182 and 3183. He sits nexts to the plumpest and tenderest hen and 'desireth most to have hire presence', as in *The Nun's Priest's Tale* 3167-9, and in the morning pays her loving attention so as to mate with her, as at lines 3177-9. As a lover and a warrior he defends his wives bravely, especially his favourite, and his courageous behaviour is the result of his choleric temperament. Both the cock's singing and his sharp sight are noted and his pride and warlike qualities were well known.

Thus, throughout the tale, the animal behaviour is maintained and against this is set the discussion between the cock and the hen and the

*Lalia Phipps Boone, 'Chauntecleer and Partlet identified' *Modern Language Notes*, LXIV, 1949, pp.78–81.

tricks which end the story. The discussion arises in a natural manner when Chauntecleer is found sitting on his perch surrounded by 'his wyves' but next to his favourite, 'faire Pertelote'. By the use of the word 'wyves' the characteristic relationship which we see acted out in the following debate is introduced. However, matrimony as an institution does not apply to chickens, only to human beings, and the joke is emphasised by using the plural form 'wyves'. According to the Christian faith men and women are allowed only one spouse at a time, but then poultry are neither Christian nor subject to social institutions such as marriage.

The courteous behaviour of the birds is shown from the opening speeches of Chauntecleer and Pertelote. Frightened by his groans Pertelote, full of concern, tenderly asks her 'herte deere' what is the matter with him. The second person plural pronoun 'ye, yow' is used throughout the discussion. The birds do not use the familiar forms 'thou, thee' but the formal, polite plural form which shows their gentility of breeding and exquisite manners. Chauntecleer's dignified answer does not conceal his fear. Although he begins decorously with a concerned expression for Pertelote's reaction, he is afraid, as his plea to God to keep him from mischief suggests. The cock's egoism is reflected in the repeated use of 'I', 'me', 'myn' and the formal way in which he recounts the dream suggests Chauntecleer's pompous nature.

Pertelote's reaction is what we would expect from a lady who has learnt that her brave hero is not as brave as she thought him. His cowardice has destroyed her love, for only brave, generous and discreet husbands are worthy of love. Having been described as a courtly lady, lines 2869–75, she reacts as such to her husband's fear. She describes in detail the ideal husband required by such courtly ladies, an ideal which, as a cock, Chauntecleer cannot achieve. The sentiments of the speech would be appropriate for a human heroine but the audience must not forget that the protagonists are birds. Line 2920 shocks us into realising that, although Chauntecleer may have a feathery beard, he cannot have a man's heart and courage. Pertelote's indignation and disappointment are aroused further by the cause of her Chauntecleer's fear—a dream—for it is well known that dreams are meaningless and only caused by bodily disorders. This firm stand taken on the worthless nature of dreams introduces the central discussion of dreams, which forms Chaucer's main addition to the first part of the poem.

The introduction of the dream motif into the story seems to have occurred in the French poem, *Le Roman de Renard*, and it is from this that Chaucer develops the long discussion on dreams and their meanings, which displays so skilfully the contrasing natures and attitudes of the two birds. In expanding this particular topic Chaucer reveals both his own interest and reading. Throughout his poetry Chaucer demonstrates an interest in dreams, their causes and significance. In this he was reflecting a contemporary preoccupation, for the explanation and meaning of dreams were important not only as a possible method of interpreting the future but as a means of diagnosing illness. As an author Chaucer's interest was probably stimulated by the use of a form of narrative now called dream-vision poetry. This genre of poetry, in which the poet falls asleep and dreams a dream, was copied by English poets from French models and Chaucer's early poetry, *The Book of the Duchess*, *The House of Fame* and *The Parliament of Fowls* are all composed as dream visions as is a later poem, *The Legend of Good Women*. Not only do these poems recount a dream but often the narrator discusses the nature of sleep and dreams as an introduction to the dream: *The Book of the Duchess* 1–43 and 221–90, *The House of Fame* 1–110, *The Parliament of Fowls* 29–112. In other poems which are not dream-visions, dreams are significant as, for example, in *Troilus and Criseyde*.

There were many authoritative writings on dreams and their interpretation available to a medieval author, but Chaucer's main source of information seems to have been an early fifth-century commentary written by Macrobius on a work, *Somnium Scipionis*, by the Roman author, Cicero. Macrobius categorised those dreams which come in sleep into five principal types, as follows:

somnium: a dream which foretells the future, but in a hidden way through allegory which needs interpretation

visio: a dream which shows events exactly as they are to happen

oraculum: a dream in which an important person, a god, or possibly a relative appears to the dreamer and advises about future conduct

insomnium: a meaningless dream, making no sense when awake

phantasma: a meaningless dream which comes to the dreamer between wakening and sleep in which vague, terrifying shapes appear

From this simple explanation it is clear that it was important to determine to which category Chauntecleer's dream belonged in order to decide whether it was a significant dream of future events or a meaningless 'insomnium' or 'phantasma'.

In his commentary Macrobius makes no comment upon dreams thought to be produced by bodily disorders or temperament and for this kind of explanation Chaucer would have had to know various medical opinions. Such opinions were based upon the medieval idea of the human body, influenced both at birth and throughout life by external forces such as the planets and internally by the mixture and balance of four components known as the humours. The world, according to medieval interpretation, was composed of the four contraries—hot, cold, dry, moist—which combine to create the four elements of fire (hot and dry), air (hot and moist), earth (cold and dry) and water (cold and moist). These four contraries combine in the human body to produce humours or bodily moistures: choler (hot and dry), blood (hot and moist), melancholy (cold and dry) and phlegm (cold and moist). Differences in human temperament were attributed to the predominance of a humour and led to the classification of human beings into the choleric nature, the sanguine nature, the melancholic nature and the phlegmatic nature. Illnesses were thought to occur from an imbalance in the humours, which would show itself in dreams. If properly understood, these dreams would show which humour predominated and needed treatment. Such a dream, called a 'somnium naturale', had no meaning except as a method of determining what was wrong with the sufferer. The other types of dreams recognised by medical opinion were the 'somnium animale', which reflected the concerns of the dreamer when awake and the 'somnium coeleste', in which the mind of the dreamer, according to its receptiveness, received impressions from celestial spirits.

With this knowledge in mind, a consideration of the discussion of Chauntecleer and Pertelote on dreams demonstrates Chaucer's learning on the topic and the use to which he puts it in the delineation of the birds' characters. For it is obvious, even from this brief account, that accurate determination of the cause and nature of a dream was not possible until, or if, the event occurred. In *The Nun's Priest's Tale*, Chaucer exploits this impossibility of accurate decision in his presentation of the birds and their behaviour as husband and wife.

Returning to the tale we see that Pertelote is convinced that dreams are 'vanitee', illusions which have no meaning. The cause of Chauntecleer's dream is an excess of red choler and melancholy, which has resulted in the dream of a red animal with black markings. To relieve the excess and to prevent a more serious illness, Chauntecleer must take a laxative to purge his stomach and bowels, preceded by a digestive of worms. In this long speech, Pertelote's single utterance, the character of the hen is presented with clarity and humour. Although she reacts exquisitely to her husband's fear, her practical nature asserts itself and she takes charge to cure her lord, not as a mistress curing her lover by granting her love, but as a wife not wanting the inconvenience of a sick husband. From the initial indignant 'fy on yow, herteless!' of the beloved, her speech becomes full of medical knowledge and erudition and ends with the triumphant, homely instruction 'Pekke hem up right as they growe and ete hem yn'. Having reacted as the injured lover, she becomes the practical, learned diagnostician and doctor. Her confidence in her opinion of the dream as a 'somnium naturale' is shown by the assertion of lines 2923–25 and the pedantic balance of the effects of choler, lines 2926–32, and of the effects of melancholy, lines 2933–36. Her exactness is suggested by the repetition of 'of . . .', such an impression being created in a similar fashion by the list of herbs, lines 2963–66. Her deference to Chauntecleer is suggested by 'pardee' (2928). Lines 2937–39 show her smug common sense in not overwhelming her husband with her erudition, although she cannot resist a reference to Cato to end her display of learning.

The tone of the next section is one of encouragement and cheerful concern. Having satisfactorily diagnosed the cause, the cure follows. Pertelote is the instructor and Chauntecleer the instructed. Lines 2942–53 are concerned with exhortation. The imperative 'For Goddes love, as taak som laxatyf' is followed by reassurances of Pertelote's good faith. Her own guidance will result in the purge. Lines 2954–67 open with a second instruction, 'Foryet nat this, for Goddes owene love!', to be careful not to develop a more serious complaint, which is followed by the list of plant purges. The speech ends with a gay demand to do as he is told and no more dreams will alarm him.

The speech reflects three aspects of Pertelote's character: the affronted lover, the learned lady, and the concerned and encouraging wife. The comforting, fussy nature of the final section, with its hints of colloquial speech, seems the most appropriate to the nature of a hen and the conviction of her own correctness and her instructions suggest the relationship of husband and wife, almost mother and child, and reflect the domestic qualities of the hen coop and the house.

It is convincing that such a practical attitude to his dream offends Chauntecleer's sensibility and masculine pride. Chauntecleer's self-esteem is such that he is convinced that he is the recipient of an important dream foretelling the future and, to support his argument and to reprove Pertelote, he quotes at length other prophetic dreams. In this way the narrator is able to widen the discussion of dreams, include other stories, and demonstrate the pedantic and self-important nature of Chauntecleer.

The form of Chauntecleer's speech is rather like that of a sermon, for he wishes to demonstrate a premise and this he does in the manner of a preacher. Chauntecleer maintains that dreams are prophetic and proves this with examples of prophetic dreams. Most of the examples end tragically with the dreamers ignoring the warnings of the dream and it is ironic that Chauntecleer presents them as evidence for the truthfulness of dreams. Although true, the dreams are ignored. Such is Chauntecleer's own behaviour, for, whilst arguing for the veracity of his dream, he cannot recognise the danger shown him in his 'visio' when he does come face to face with Russell. The tragic tales told by Chauntecleer maintain the human dimension in the story and offer a contrasting mood. The sombre accounts of human folly and death contrast with the comic situation of the poultry. Chauntecleer's egoism is shown by the earnest seriousness with which he treats his dream, a failing shared by many. Although they are tragic tales, their use is comic as they serve to emphasise the conceit of Chauntecleer.

Chauntecleer's speech is an account of the stories, interspersed with comments. His pompous introduction, lines 2970–83, asserts his masculine superiority and wider erudition. The pained irony of 'graunt mercy of youre loore' is followed by the dismissal of Pertelote's authority. Cato, by the opinions of anonymous men 'moore of auctorite'. Conceit is suggested by the polysyllabic words 'sentence', 'experience', 'significaciouns', 'tribulaciouns', 'argument', more abstract concepts in contrast to Pertelote's practicality. The classical stories are recounted in a lively manner holding the attention but it is Chauntecleer's comments which are revealing. The pompous moralising on divine justice of lines 3050–57 is irrelevant, as murder is not the issue. Chauntecleer has been carried away by the force of his own words. This increasing involvement in his subject is shown throughout the rest of the speech by the use of familiar, colloquial phrases. Lines 3063–66 and 3105–9 show this tone as does 'Noot I nat why' (3100), 'faire Pertelote' (3105), 'for I seye thee, doutelees' (3108), lines 3120–1, lines 3122, 'I pray yow' (3127), 'I sey nat alle' (3131) and others. Intellectually convinced that he 'shal han of this avisioun/Adversitee' (3152–3), Chauntecleer refuses to take any laxatives as he dislikes them. The climax of the erudite list of classical, biblical and native stories is an expression of distaste!

In the last section, 3157–71, Chauntecleer attempts to mollify Pertelote. Having established his intellectual superiority, Chauntecleer becomes the lover, flattering 'Madame Pertelote', praising her beauty and ready to face all dangers emboldened by his enjoyment of her. To combine both erudition and flattery Chauntecleer includes a Latin tag which he mistranslates. Its true meaning 'From the beginning woman is man's confusion' refers obliquely to the biblical story of Adam and Eve and the expulsion of mankind from Paradise by eating the fruit of the tree of knowledge. Chauntecleer mistranslates this tag as 'Woman is man's joy and all his happiness'. Whether Chauntecleer is mistranslating to flatter Pertelote or whether he does not know he is wrong is left unclear. In a sense Chauntecleer's mistranslation heightens the joke, for it is possible that in some scales of value woman is man's joy and bliss and also his ruin.

In contrast to Pertelote's speech, Chauntecleer has changed from superior teacher to flattering lover, concerned that he may be denied his physical pleasures. Chauntecleer forgets his fear in his exuberant behaviour as a lover, encouraged by the romantic season of spring. But, as 'the latter ende of joye is wo' (3205), Chauntecleer's happy mood gives way to one of foreboding, on which the narrator comments. Having introduced the fox, the narrator returns to the happy behaviour of the birds, and he is careful to establish both the avian and human aspects of Chauntecleer's characterisation, for it is as a cock and as a quasi-human being that Chauntecleer must respond. This is done by commenting on the hens taking a sand bath, an avian pastime, and by commenting on Chauntecleer's singing. The comparison made is with mermaids, half-human, half-fish creatures who lured sailors to their deaths by singing so enticingly that ships were wrecked on the rocks. The narrator, by using the figure of the mermaid, suggests the hybrid nature of the mythical beings, a hybrid nature which is present in the characterisation of Chauntecleer.

On meeting the fox Chauntecleer's reaction is instinctive fear for, as is pointed out, all creatures flee their enemies even if they have not seen them before with their own eyes. The humour is that whilst Chauntecleer behaves as a cock who has never seen a fox, he has seen a fox in his dream and has spent some time convincing Pertelote that his dream foretold the future. He has 'seen' the fox in his mind's eye but his learning fails him in the application of the lesson of his dream. Forgetting the dream's warning, of which he was convinced only a short time before, Chauntecleer is an easy victim to the fox's winning ways. The gullible, self-important bird believes what the fox says for, like all vain people, he wants to believe the compliments. Ravished by the flattery he succumbs to Russell's trick and, once his eyes are closed, he is seized by the fox.

In the chase the audience's attention is concentrated on the pursuers and when the tale returns to the pursuit the time elapsed has made it possible for the cock to plan a trick. Chauntecleer, despite his fear, tricks the fox into opening his mouth to boast of his triumph to the following crowd. Refusing to be enticed by the fox's sweet talk twice, Chauntecleer's contempt for himself and the fox is shown by the bluntness of speech and the use of the second person singular pronoun. Chauntecleer draws the moral that he will not succumb to flattery, for all must remain alert against such trickery.

Thus the narrator conveys the character of a vain, silly, pretentious cock whose learning proves no use to him. Through the descriptions of Chauntecleer as a noble, as a lover, and as a conscious scholar, the narrator conveys the behaviour of the cock with reference to human attributes, thus comically telling us about both Chauntecleer and human nature. Similarly in the presentation of Pertelote as lady, beloved, and wife, a comment upon feminine nature is made as well.

The final major animal character is Russell, who provides the action in the tale. In his presentation of the fox, as with Chauntecleer, the narrator expands the attributes of cunning and deceit traditionally associated with the animal.

In *Le Roman de Renard* the fox appears before the dream and the accurate interpretation of the allegorical dream-animal as a fox is given after the hens have seen the animal, Chauntecler's folly being shown by his ignoring of the plain truth. In *The Nun's Priest's Tale* the description of the animal in the dream is given before the appearance of the fox and is not identified as a fox, Pertelote being too concerned that Chauntecleer is a coward and Chauntecleer too concerned to defend the gravity of his dream. Chauntecleer is shown to ignore his own advice, not that of Pertelote's mistaken interpretation. Although the fox is described, he is not identified and this lack of identification fits in with Chauntecleer's incapacity to acknowledge his instinctive distrust of the fox. We, the audience, know from the description it is a fox; Chauntecleer knows from his dream that the creature wishes him harm but Chauntecleer has no intellectual identification of the fox, only an instinctive fear, which is appropriate for a cock.

Through the dream description Russell is introduced into the tale early but he is forgotten in the dispute over dreams. With his active introduction at line 3215 we learn that the fox is 'ful of sly iniquitee'. The narrator likens his deception to three famous betrayals, the most profound being the betrayal of Christ by Judas Iscariot. Having established the fox's notable, if disreputable, human counterparts, we see the cunning fox at work. Recognising Chauntecleer's understandable fear the fox hastens to reassure the cock. Addressing him courteously as 'gentil sire' and with the use of the second person plural pronoun, Russell assures Chauntecleer that his errand is not one of danger to the cock but rather a cause of pride. The word 'allas', the innocent questions 'wher wol ye gon?' and 'Be ye affrayed of me that am youre freend?', and the soothing statement that the fox would be a real villain if he wished to harm the cock, suggest the preposterous nature of such an idea. The mood of false security is maintained by the use of 'trewely' (lines 3289, 3291) to give the impression of sincerity. Through the traditional attributes of deceit and cunning, the audience recognises that the fox's words do not mean what they appear to mean and what the gullible Chauntecleer believes. The fox's words suggest a humble, conciliatory manner for 'allas', 'trewely', 'God his soule blesse!' (3295), and line 3298 gives the impression of a person trying to please, but this impression is played off against the audience's knowledge. References to Chauntecleer's parents convey a double meaning for although they have been to Russell's house, it is as food not as visitors.

The subject of Russell's flattery appeals to Chauntecleer's vanity. It is Chauntecleer's fame as a singer which has encouraged the fox to visit, for the cock sings like an angel and is superior in musical sensitivity to the authority, Boethius. The fox praises Chauntecleer's father who, with the exception of Chauntecleer, was the best singer amongst men! The tone of the fox's flattery is conveyed through the repeated use of 'he' referring to Chauntecleer's father (3303, 3305, 3306, 3309), the repeated use of 'his' (3304, 3305, 3307, 3308), and the use of 'and', all of which concentrate our attention upon Chauntecleer's father and increase our expectations as one detail is added to another. The fox's description visualises the cock's behaviour and we accept the absurd claim

'that ther nas no man in no regioun
That hym in song or wisdom myghte passe'

as does Chauntecleer. Having lulled Chauntecleer into a false sense of security with these familiar and flattering references to his family, the fox asks Chauntecleer to emulate his father.

The narrator conveys the character of the fox by assuming that, with their knowledge of the sly fox, the audience can enjoy the humour of the situation and almost side with the clever fox against the stupid cock. For Russell uses some of the techniques which Chauntecleer used in his discussion with Pertelote and this time they show Chauntecleer's limitations. Russell makes learned references to Boethius and the book of 'Daun Burnel the Asse' and tells a story to illustrate his persuasive argument. The familiarity of tone and the references to Chauntecleer's family suggest intimacy, yet throughout Russell is deferential in his manner to the cock. Thus the narrator provides the fox with a typical 'foxy' nature but he is careful to maintain the human references to provide the dual applicability. Russell has a house, is interested in singing, reading, popular opinion and learned debate, and his references to families are appropriate in a human social setting not an animal one.

Having seized Chauntecleer and run off Russell falls prey to the same vice, vanity, which has enabled him to trick the cock. Never a creature to give up, Russell attempts to entice the cock again using the same technique and verbal manner. 'Allas' (3419), 'sire' (3423), 'God help me so!' (3425) suggest deference, and concern is shown by Russell assuming the blame for the misunderstanding 'I have to yow' (3420), 'I maked yow' (3421), 'I yow hente' (3422) and the conviction of 'I shal seye sooth to yow' (3425). Chauntecleer is not to be tricked twice and, bereft of his meal, Russell draws the apposite conclusion.

So all the major, named characters in the tale are animals, but animals with human qualities and natures through whose behaviour something can be learnt by man. However the story is given a human framework and there remain two participants on which to comment. First is the poor widow whose description opens the tale. She is a passive character taking no effective part in the action, as even the rescue of Chauntecleer is achieved by his own wits and not human intervention. She serves as a contrast to Chauntecleer in the descriptions but also as a discreet scale of reference for the birds' behaviour. Always, in the back of our minds is the knowledge that Chauntecleer and Pertelote are only birds and that they are owned by the widow. Although she is less effectively and lavishly presented, although she takes a limited part in the tale, she is human and ultimately the example against which the quasi-human behaviour of the poultry must be measured.

The other important voice is that of the tale's narrator, which leads into a discussion of the style of *The Nun's Priest's Tale*.

Style

Throughout the discussion of character much has been said on the question of style, as characterisation in this tale is presented, at least in part, by the manipulations of style. The characters of Chauntecleer and Pertelote are presented in description and action through the use of words and concepts more properly used in romances telling the adventures of heroes and ladies. This stylistic use provides humour, for there is something comic in presenting the actions of birds as though they are important and significant and presenting this in a serious manner by the use of certain styles. The comedy arises from the inappropriateness of this kind of description, but also the realisation of the almost correct use of the style. If birds and animals can be used to represent human beings, then their actions are important in so far as they have significance for human beings, but they are not important if applied to birds. This burlesquing of noble concepts and actions in the mock-heroic style is conveyed deftly by Chaucer and we enjoy it for the humour and the skill with which it is presented. In other works Chaucer uses such noble sentiments and attitudes seriously and with dignity and it is an indication of Chaucer's poetic maturity that, in addition, he is able to use such ideas comically.

However, much of the atmosphere and emphasis of the poem is conveyed by the intervention and control of the narrator. It is a vexed critical question as to whether the narrator represents the feelings and attitudes of the Nun's Priest or whether it is Chaucer the author telling another tale. In the telling of the tale there is nothing to prevent the first of these possibilities from being true, as the tone, content, and style would be appropriate for a cleric, but as we have no characterisation of the Nun's Priest, apart from what can be inferred from the tale and the Host's remarks in the Prologue and Epilogue to the tale, there is little support for this idea. The narrator may represent the Nun's Priest, but equally he may not be intended as a character-sketch of the pilgrim. If we approach the narrator as an element in the style of the tale, the problem may not appear so significant.

In the opening passage the narrator makes two comments: line 2824 'of which I telle yow my tale', which suggests initially that the tale is to be of the widow, and lines 2880–81 in which the narrator emphasises the fable nature of the story by referring to talking birds and beasts. Here the narrator is joking slyly for he maintains that birds and beasts could talk at 'thilke tyme', thus extending the stylistic device to a claim of truth.

The major contribution of the narrator to the tale's tone occurs after the birds' discussion and, through the use of various stylistic devices, the action of the plot is delayed further and the suspense increased. Also the mock-heroic tone of the poem is intensified. This is achieved by the use of certain rhetorical devices. In the Middle Ages rhetoric was the art of composition, and to assist authors numerous handbooks were written describing the manner in which stories should be structured, the management of descriptions and the many ways of elaborating a story according to its type and purpose. In his poetry Chaucer makes use of this instruction but as he became a more mature and confident writer, Chaucer, whilst using rhetorical principles seriously, also put them to comic effect. This is noticeable particularly when the story is either comically elevated or diminished by the inclusion of rhetorical devices, which are not suitable to the story's material. Such a method is used in *The Nun's Priest's Tale* through the medium of the narrator.

The four main figures of embellishment demonstrated in the narrator's comments are circumlocutio, exclamatio, digressio and collatio, all of which elaborate this tale for comic purposes. Circumlocutio can be seen at lines 3187–97 in which a simple fact, the time and day of the month, is conveyed in complex and grand language. The importance of the day is indicated but, as it is an important day only for a bird, the grand manner is used comically. The use of exclamatio is evidenced at lines 3226–29 where the delaying, intensifying apostrophe suggests a connection between the fox, acting according to his nature, and human traitors, who are betraying their own kind. This heightening of feeling is comic, for in reality Russell has no connection with Judas, Ganelon and Sinon, except in literature. The third figure, digressio, arises from the following exclamatio of lines 3230–3. The discussion of predestination is an amplification of an idea within the story and demonstrates one kind of digressio. The very introduction of such a serious human topic in the discussion of a cock's behaviour is, in itself, comic and the narrator draws attention to its inappropriateness by breaking off at line 3251

I wol nat han to do of swich mateere;
My tale is of a cok, as ye may heere,

but then being caught up in another short digressio. The fourth figure, collatio or comparison, can be seen in the description of Chauntecleer and that of the shrieking hens.

The use of these figures helps to delay the action, widen the reference of the poem and, above all, alter the tone of the poem. By their inclusion the poem becomes, in part, a literary joke. Such figures are used correctly at the appropriate moments, but their subject is the behaviour of poultry and, as such, the figures heighten the humour and absurdity of the application. Some critics believe that Chaucer is ridiculing rhetorical practice, but the effect is rather of affectionate playfulness. Chaucer is well aware of the danger of such rules, but he does use them seriously in some poems, whilst displaying, as here, the comic use to which such precepts can be put. As an author he can rely upon his audience's knowledge of the appropriate use and their recognition of the comic application in this tale.

The narrator's delaying tactics are seen clearly in the poem's second section. The circumlocutio of lines 3187–97 is followed by a brief reference to the poultry, but then by a moralising statement on the transience of earthly joy, a serious topic. However, the narrator alters our mood by maintaining that his story is as true as that of Sir Lancelot.

He throws our certainty into doubt by suggesting that it is women who esteem such tales, women who, it is implied, are gullible. Humorously the narrator queries the seriousness of his own tale. Similarly in the following verse paragraph, there is a section of story with the introduction of Russell at lines 3215–25, and then the narrator proceeds, via exclamatio and digressio, to delay the action and heighten the suspense.

The exclamatio of lines 3225–29 and 3230–33 lead into the digressio on human predestination, a subject suitable for a cleric. Curtailing this discussion, he comments on Chauntecleer's stupid behaviour in accepting his wife's advice. This suggests to the narrator another example of man's folly in listening to a woman, for Eve's enticement bereft Adam of Paradise. Conscious that such defamation of women may displease some of his audience, he refers them to other opinions and claims the words are Chauntecleer's, not his. This passage brings together many of the tale's themes, that of predestination, that of the relationship in marriage, that of the authority of books and sages. The digression delays the action, reflects the narrator's concerns and adds a relevant human aspect to the tale.

The learned asides of lines 3271–2 and 3279–81 do not delay progress for long and Russell flatters the silly cock. Picking up the theme of flattery, the narrator indulges in a solemn warning. Again he is tantalising his audience, delaying our knowledge of what Chauntecleer will do, for although the figure is rhetorically correct, its inclusion creates suspense. The next seven lines are the only lines which forward the action in the section 3325–74, the remainder being examples of exclamatio and collatio, which increase the mock-heroic tone, provide humour, and abandon Chauntecleer. Between his capture at line 3325 and the chase at line 3375, the action of the story is suspended. The exclamatio to destiny, Venus and Geoffrey de Vinsauf and the collatio on the frightened hens heighten the pathos and emotion. The hero's fate and the heroine's reactions are properly recorded and the mock-heroic tone is maintained and the humour increased.

From lines 3187 to 3375 the use of rhetorical figures is manipulated to delay the action, alter the tone, and sustain the humour of the poem. The poem's scope is widened by the inclusion of learned material and discussion, as the first part of the poem has been. Rhetoric is used accurately but for mock-heroic effect and the burlesque and the fun are products of a sophisticated literary usage.

The narrator does not intrude in the chase or in the final reversal of fortunes, although at lines 3402 to 3404 he prepares us for the denouement. He does have the last word, however. Both the cock and the fox draw their own morals, their own reactions to the events, but the narrator, too, wishes to emphasise a moral conclusion. Addressing his audience for the last time, he warns them not to dismiss the tale as an amusing, senseless 'folye'. As with many apparently innocent and simple stories, there is a deeper and more significant understanding to be gained, if the audience will consider the tale more philosophically. Lines 3436–37 give an obvious moral but a more subtle meaning, 'the fruyt', will yield the truth if 'the chaf' is disregarded. However, as with the rest of the tale, the ending remains tantalising and ambiguous because the narrator does not clearly state what is 'the chaf' in the tale and what, more importantly, is 'the fruyt'. The meaning of the tale remains for each reader to decide and this freedom accounts, in part, for the tale's charm and attraction. It is a comic tale and solemn moralising would be inappropriate, but there is a serious moral to be gained if the tale is read aright and this will enhance, not spoil, the comedy. This freedom of interpretation has meant that critics have been, still are and will go on offering many explanations of the tale and it is with a brief consideration of these that this section will conclude.

The main critical concerns fall into three groups: firstly, those interpretations of the tale which are concerned with its meaning as biblical allegory; secondly, those interpretations which are interested in the teller of the tale; thirdly, those interpretations concerned with the literary form of the tale.

Those critics who hold the first view wish to interpret the tale as having a Christian significance. The fox is seen as a symbol of the devil who tricks the cock, a symbol of the good man or even a cleric. When Chauntecleer resorts to reason, having rejected flattery, he is saved. Chauntecleer's fault is to deny his reason and to succumb, first, to the fleshly desire for Pertelote and, then, to flattery. The poor widow is the symbol of all that is good, sometimes considered as the Church, and her simplicity and life of denial are an example to the audience. Certain critics have seen Chauntecleer's capture and escape as a comic symbol of Adam's fall and redemption.

The second critical opinion is shown by those critics who attempt to construct a character for the Nun's Priest from the Host's remarks and from the tale. The themes of the tale reflect the cleric occupation of the teller and the anti-feminist remarks demonstrate his dislike of his superior, the Prioress. Another critic sees the tale as a warning to the Monk. The Monk will come to 'a sticky end' if he continues to put worldly pleasures before his monastic duties.

Finally, there are those critics who are interested in the literary form of the tale. Chaucer's knowledge of rhetoric is rejected by one critic who believes that such information on figures could have been learnt from contemporary grammars. Another critic sees the tale as an anti-fable, confirmed as such because we are asked to draw our own moral. Similarly Chaucer is seen to be making fun of rhetorical instructions by his comic use of them. Connections with other stories in *The Canterbury Tales* are made, especially with *The Monk's Tale*.

So the tale is an allegory, a character-sketch or a literary joke and its moral is Christian, personal or of literary implications. At the end of the Prologue to *The Miller's Tale* the narrator states

Avyseth yow, and put me out of blame;
And eek men shal nat maken ernest of game.

Such a warning may well apply to *The Nun's Priest's Tale*. Whilst we must decide for ourselves what is 'the fruyt' and what 'the chaf', whilst we must recognise the serious implications of the tale for human behaviour, we can also admire and delight in the humour and elegance of the tale. As the definition of 'fruyt' and 'chaf' can never be decided absolutely, the earnestness of the game should not be pursued too far.

Part 4

Hints for study

General points

On a first reading the tale will, doubtless, seem very strange. Not only is it in a foreign language, but it is in a form of that language which is no longer used today. Such difficulties are faced by all readers, whether they are native English speakers or not. In studying all early literature there are problems of linguistic and cultural differences and we must be sensitive to these so that we do not misinterpret the author's intentions.

Vocabulary

The immediate difficulties are the vocabulary, the syntax, and the unfamiliar intellectual concepts, such as the astrological details and the medical lore. The only way to combat these problems is to become familiar with the text. This means reading the text carefully with all notes and glossaries until you understand the meanings of the words and concepts used. At this first stage do not worry about the interpretations and meaning of the tale, but aim to be able to understand the text, eventually without any aids. It may be helpful to transcribe the tale into a modern English form, as this will familiarise you with the structure of the tale. However, no modern adaptation, either your own or someone else's, can replace the original and your ambition must be to read the tale in its Middle English form with ease and assurance. All notes and summaries are only aids to study, and your assessment and appreciation of the work must be based upon your own familiarity with it.

The problem of vocabulary and lexical meaning is best overcome by looking at the words in their context. There is no point in making lists of strange words and attempting to learn them out of context. The meaning and nuance of the meaning depends in part on the situation in which the word is being used. Constant re-reading will make the form and the meaning of the words clear. Particular care should be taken with those words which appear to have a modern English form but whose lexical meaning has altered. If you are asked to translate a section of the tale from Middle English into a modern language, try and convey the differences of style which appear in the original. In the description of Chauntecleer and the hens, much of the humour is conveyed by the use of romance vocabulary, not normally applied to chickens. Try and reflect this in your own translation by choosing ¹ignified and elegant equivalents. It will not always be possible to have a one to one equivalent, and then the meaning must be conveyed by the use of a phrase. Modern English has lost some of the lexical subtleties of Middle English as, for example, the distinction in the pronoun of address. Modern English 'you' does not distinguish between a polite and an intimate usage and is, therefore, poorer. If your own language has this flexibility, then use it, if such a translation is required.

Syntax

Although it is useful to have a knowledge of Middle English grammar in general, try to understand the various structures as they occur in the poem. If a translation is needed, then it is sometimes more elegant to alter the syntactical structure. For example 'me mette' (2894) is an impersonal construction but the meaning is conveyed more idiomatically by the personal construction, 'I dreamt'. At times, the arrangement of the sentence has an unfamiliar or clumsy feeling to a modern reader and has to be re-arranged for clearer comprehension. A point of interest is that the punctuation used in modern editions is largely editorial, as medieval manuscripts show little punctuation.

Content

The unfamiliar ideas in the tale must be understood in as far as they are relevant to the story. Medieval learning on dreams is extensive and more complicated than the notes demonstrate, but as long as you understand enough to appreciate the debate in the tale, then that is enough. If you are interested in the topic then the recommended books will help you to study the subject, but Chaucer uses only some of these ideas in this tale. The same is true of the medical remedies offered by Pertelote. Although it adds to our delighted appreciation if we know the exact plants and their effects to which she refers, the lists are meant to tell us more about Pertelote's concern and worry. Her practical knowledge and experience is contrasted with Chauntecleer's book learning.

Such a familiarity with the text and the elements of the story is the first concern and it is not until this has been done that it is advisable to read any interpretative works on the tale. Critical scholarship on Chaucer's works is sophisticated and can be confusing to the reader who is beginning his study. The introduction to the editions mentioned in the reading list and those books suggested as background reading should be consulted first. After becoming familiar with the text, try and make up your own mind as to the tale's meaning, then read other interpretations of the tale, which may challenge or confirm your own opinions. If your own view can be supported from evidence in the text, is a cohesive and logical argument, then retain it. Much criticism is personal opinion, and often a careful, detailed knowledge of the text produces a clearer critical understanding.

Points of detail

Having gained such an assurance, then a more sophisticated approach to the tale will suggest itself to the reader. The tale can be appreciated for its details of style and structure, the development of character, and the presentation of ideas.

Structure

In dealing with questions of structure, the following points should be considered: the episodes into which the tale can be divided; the comparative length and importance of these episodes; the contrasting tone and atmosphere. The introductory portrait of the widow gives the human background against which the brilliant birds can act. This introduction is short, negative and the widow is only described. In contrast, in the episode of Chauntecleer and Pertelote, we are told their description and then their own behaviour is shown in the debate. Although this long section is a conversation, Chauntecleer's speech is a series of narratives demonstrating Chaucer's ability to tell short stories within the framework of a story. The introduction of Russell and the narrator's additions follow, introducing a reflective and philosophical tone. The character of the fox is demonstrated in his speech and, after the capture, rhetorical figures are introduced. This elevated section is followed by the intense and vivid activity of the chase, which contrasts with the intimate conversation between Chauntecleer and the fox. The poem ends with a direct address to the audience, making the moral decision theirs. So the structuring of the tale presents contrasting episodes of narrative and conversation, activity and rhetoric, description and comment, all of varying lengths and importance. Questions on structure may well involve the purpose of the so-called digressions of the narrator and the length of Chauntecleer's contribution to the debate, as well as the effect of the delaying of the action. An attempt has been made in Part 3 to show that the rhetorical fire-works of the narrator are necessary to elevate and deflate the tone of the poem and to delay the action further and tantalise the audience more. Chauntecleer's series of stories also delays the action but it also displays the pedantic character of the bird. The postponement of the activity until the end of the tale allows the discussion of interesting topics, which portrays the actors and display Chaucer's learning in a humorous fashion. The audience is asked to enjoy the method of getting to the end. If the outcome of the story is known, then the audience has the time and the capacity to appreciate other aspects developed by the author. Nevertheless, the tension does mount at the end of the story, so Chaucer's presentation includes both reflection and expansion and the suspense needed to sustain the plot.

Characterisation

The question of characterisation is fundamental to any discussion of the tale. *The Nun's Priest's Tale* does not show the development of character as do plays or novels. Rather we are shown the characters behaving in a certain fashion and their personalities are expanded by the style in which additional comments are made. We are presented with the actors in the story, the cock, hen, and fox, and the author builds upon our ordinary knowledge of these creatures with the extraordinary attributes with which he endows them. We are all familiar with the behaviour of poultry, the apparently aggressive and proud bearing of a cock, the comfortable domestic qualities of a hen. Foxes, too, have traditional associations with cunning and deceit, with skill and elegant appearance. Many of these qualities are shown in the tale but, to these well-known aspects are added refinements.

Through the method of stylistic description, the qualities of warrior and lover are added to Chauntecleer and the qualities of lady and beloved to Pertelote. The use of vocabulary by the narrator in his descriptions adds these further dimensions. In the behaviour of the birds themselves we see the elegant manners and loving behaviour. The human relationship of marriage increases the range of possible behavioural and emotional aspects. In the characterisation of Chauntecleer and Pertelote we are shown two contrasting personalities, both restrained by the same code of genteel behaviour, but remaining true to their fundamental nature, that of poultry. Description, behaviour and way of speech demonstrate the characters of the birds.

Detailed examination of the character of Pertelote

In considering questions of characterisation, you should exemplify these general comments with close reference to the text. For example, in considering the character of Pertelote we must look at all the references made to her as well as her own speech. She is shown as a hen, a lover and a wife. The heroine of the story, she is introduced after the hero. By the portrait of Chauntecleer we realise that the birds are not only birds, but something rather unusual. Chauntecleer is a superlative cock but it is with the introduction of Pertelote that finer feelings, sentiments and behaviour are mentioned. She is described as one of 'sevene hennes', who are the 'sustres and paramours' of Chauntecleer, a comment combining both human and avian references. The 'faire damoysele Pertelote' is 'curteys', 'discreet, and debonaire' and her charming behaviour has enslaved the hero, Chauntecleer. Thus the initial aspect of Pertelote and her relationship with Chauntecleer is that of the heroine of the story, the beloved whose attraction is supreme.

Pertelote, as Chauntecleer's favourite, has the place next to him on the perch and it is to her that he turns when troubled. In her first reaction to the dream we are shown Pertelote's refined sensibilities and her reference to female opinion show her to have a ladylike personality. However, this attitude alters when her practical concern and wifely interest overcome her elegance. Her experience and learning are demonstrated by her remedies, and her encouragement to Chauntecleer shows her fond and straightforward attitude towards her Chauntecleer—she is not afraid of this imposing cock. So we are presented with a personality in which the bird qualities are not emphasised. Later she takes a sand bath, and her beauty is definitely that of a hen, but her character of lover and wife is what is stressed. Although she does not speak again, we learn more of her through Chauntecleer's attitude and narratorial comment. Chauntecleer shows his own superiority and disdain for Pertelote by his display of greater learning and Pertelote's diagnoses is indeed wrong. But the cock's flattering references and subsequent attentions show Pertelote's charms as a lover and a hen. Women should charm and please, not be clever and lecture! The last reference to her ennobles her in her capacity as a distressed wife. The rhetorical exaggeration of the narrator likening the hens to famous human wives is both funny and ridiculous. Yet it sustains the characterisation of Pertelote as a concerned wife which, as we have seen, is the dominant feature.

The mixture of human and animal behaviour, partly described and partly acted, is true also of the personalities of Chauntecleer and

Russell. They are creatures, plus human attributes, attitudes and social responses, which are conveyed through vocabulary, tone and action. The character of the narrator can also be shown if you think that the tale is presented as a character indication of the Nun's Priest. The clerical concerns, the learned apparatus and the moral, all contribute.

Quotations

Chaucer is a narrative poet and his poetry does not lend iself to lengthy quotations. Instead try to remember phrases which you can use as illustrations within a sentence.

You should be able to discuss the vocabulary used, the figures of rhetoric and the range of learned references. The characters speak in different ways, and the narrative interludes are differently handled—think, for example, of the contrast between the description of the widow, the description of the day and the description of the chase. Both the variety of vocabulary and reference extends the limits of the story and introduce other examples, other ideas which contribute to the atmosphere and tone.

The moral of the tale

The human aspects of the characterisation enable us to apply the story to human behaviour and we are encouraged to do so by the narrator. Each reader should make up his own mind as to what the tale means and how it is to be understood. Readers will find different aspects of interest and different moral solutions. Whatever moral we arrive at, the humour, joy and elegance of the tale will remain as our chief expression. Chaucer is one of the greatest of all storytellers and he holds our interest and delight. Both as a writer and as a man, he was interested in morality, but he realised that the moral of the story is more effectively conveyed if we enjoy the story. We remember *The Nun's Priest's Tale* with affection, and then we begin to puzzle out its meaning.

Part 5

Suggestions for further reading

The text

The Complete Works of Geoffrey Chaucer, edited by F.N. Robinson, second edition, Oxford University Press, London, 1957. This volume includes all of Chaucer's accepted works and has been used throughout these notes.

The Nun's Priest Tale, edited by Nevil Coghill and Christopher Tolkien, Harrap, London, 1959.

The Nun's Priest's Tale, edited by Kenneth Sisam, Oxford University Press, Oxford, 1927.

General reading

BAUGH, ALBERT C.: *A History of the English Language*, second edition, Routlege and Kegan Paul, London, 1959.

BREWER, DEREK: *Chaucer in His Time*, Thomas Nelson and Sons, London, 1963.

BREWER, D.S.: *Chaucer*, third edition, Longman, London, 1973.

BREWER, D.S. (ED.): *Chaucer and Chaucerians*, Thomas Nelson and Sons, London, 1966.

CURRY, WALTER CLYDE: *Chaucer and the Mediaeval Sciences*, second edition, George Allen and Unwin, London, 1960.

MUSCATINE, CHARLES: *Chaucer and the French Tradition*, University of California Press, Berkeley and Los Angeles, 1969.

ROWLAND, BERYL (ED.): *Companion to Chaucer Studies*, Oxford University Press, Toronto, New York and London, 1968.

The author of these notes

The author is a graduate of the University of Newcastle on Tyne. She took a post-graduate diploma in English as a Second Language at the University of Leeds, and having completed research in Anglo-Saxon poetry at the University of Newcastle on Tyne, she taught Old and Middle English at the New University of Ulster until 1974. At present she is a tutorial assistant at the University of Dundee.

York Handbooks: list of titles

YORK HANDBOOKS form a companion series to York Notes and are designed to meet the wider needs of students of English and related fields. Each volume is a compact study of a given subject area, written by an authority with experience in communicating the essential ideas to students at all levels.